MIDNIGHT MOVERS

The unseen world of trucks at night

Accurate Dragster Publishing

MIDNIGHT MOVERS

The unseen world of trucks at night

Mark Gredzinski

Cover: This Scania 113 low datum 4x2 tractor belonging to Fagan and Whalley fitted the bill for the cover shot. The picture was a result of both good fortune and experience. It is exactly as it came out of the camera on film. Near the side of the lorry was a large illuminated poster hoarding that acted like a wide studio flash. The thin layer of snow served as a giant reflector. The moon was rendered blue by the tungsten balanced film I was using and it matched the colours on the polypipe load. The shutter speed was relatively quick at around ten seconds because there was sufficient light on the Scania. This enabled the background to quickly diminish into darkness, without being recorded.

Previous Page: February 1988 was the date for this quite new ERF E6 rigid 16 tonner operated by TNT Overnite Parcels Express. I took a few exposures and varied the length of them to make sure of success. This one would have been around ten seconds duration and the trailing car headlights recorded as a streak of light that obscured the number plate of E113 TVM. The shot was taken around rush hour in Birmingham city centre.

For Adam 'Jasper' Gredzinski
(1958 - 2016)

Always a driver, never a steering wheel attendant.

This tidy second generation Volvo F10 was operated by NT Whitfield of Stockton-on-Tees who have been in operation since 1981. The shot was taken in early 1999 when the lift axle 6x2 tractor had almost a decade of use under its wheels. A subsequent picture saw it parked next to a more modern FH12 unit in NT Whitfield's smart silver and maroon livery.

CONTENTS

In June 2013 I was compiling images for a project at Walsall College that eventually garnered me a BA Honours degree at Birmingham City University in Photography. This is one of the few digital images in this book and depicts a Volvo FM eight wheeled tipper at work from early evening throughout the night, carrying asphalt for a road resurfacing contract. The idea was to capture busy road mending activity and I got some decent images like this, hand held, without the use of a tripod. An advantage of using digital where the ISO speed rating can be useably high.

PREFACE

Writing a book about trucks is hardly a unique endeavour but one with an emphasis on night time photography probably is. The idea was to highlight the sombre and occasionally spectacular atmosphere of trucks at night. It is an unseen aspect of road haulage that occurs after every working day but is rarely recorded or appreciated. The book depicts a variety of machines from smaller rigids to heavy articulated tractors. Included are British lorries from the mid-seventies, together with their many European cousins.

Taking the pictures was often a trial. I was either on foot or for the most part, travelled by bicycle in occasional sub-zero conditions. Using colour transparency film, exposures for each picture would often run to minutes. I learned how to set up the camera and position the lens to cope with mixed artificial lighting and reflections from street lamps. Technical and physical difficulties were compounded by trying to accomplish the task on very limited funds - often during periods of unemployment.

The whole episode from humble beginnings, together with descriptions of each vehicle, is described. The book serves to be a pictorial record and is not an attempt at tales of trucking life or night trunking. Better qualified people than me – the men behind the wheel, can tell that story. The viewpoint is mine from the outside in as merely an observer, with no opportunity to stage the scene. The journey to finally achieving pictorial quality is explained with appropriate exposure details where relevant. The methods employed could be applied to any subject at night, so may be useful to any students of photography.

So why do this at all? The photography was done in isolation with no external direction or financial input. Most shots were taken without anyone's knowledge or consent. Often there was no-one to ask! The book serves to show how todays ordinary can become tomorrow's extraordinary and fundamentally I wanted to document a disappearing world. The harsh reality is that many cases, the drivers are now sadly deceased, the haulage companies are out of business, the lorry parks dug up and many truck manufacturers are now no longer with us.

However, the main consideration was that under a starlit night, the trucks just looked fabulous!

Note. No Photoshop was used to process the photographs. I used a basic program to remove any artefacts and adjust exposure or lighting anomalies. The colours are sometimes strange but that is how they were rendered on film. The pictures are therefore true to life. I hope you get the same satisfaction as I did when taking them.

Note. No sleeping driver was ever woken up by me taking these pictures. I'm proud of that fact.

PROLOGUE

It is a few minutes past midnight and I'm pacing slowly up and down the kitchen. I can't decide whether go or not, but I'm running out of excuses. The flat where I live is invitingly warm and I'm not that tired. Conditions outside however, are perfect. It's a cold, clear and importantly, a still night. The lighting mix will be just right under the moon and street lamps. I look at my bicycle once more, propped in the hall and decide to leave.

I load my careworn camera into the rucksack, along with a compact tripod, wedged diagonally to keep it from falling out. Into my pockets I stuff gloves, a balaclava and a cable release to activate the camera shutter. I gently unlock the front door and squeeze the bike through, carefully avoiding scraping the pedals on the door frame so as not to wake anyone. I wince as the latch resounds with an unavoidable 'ker-thock' as it shuts.

I'm standing on the landing of the eighth floor in a seventeen story council tower block. It smells of stale cigarette smoke, dust and years of cabbage derived cookery. I press the lift button. Above me, the electric motor whirrs into life to lower the lift cage and on arrival, the doors scrape lazily open. I'm greeted by a corner puddle of fresh neanderthal urine and the smell of disinfectant attempting to mask years of dessicated human debris. I grab the bike handlebars, elevating it to cram the front wheel into the confined corner of the muffled metal box I'm about to descend in and press 'G'.

Once on the ground floor, the doors open onto the echo chamber of the low-ceilinged vestibule. I walk across the stone floor, try not to think of the thousand tons of concrete above me and press the button to release the lock on the outside door. Once open, cold air wipes across my face, as the internal echoes evaporate into the cotton wool of a dark night. I mount my 1975 paint-chipped yellow steed and wince at the cold steel of the frame against my warm leg and coast the fifty yards to the bottom of the ramped drive. I pull the levers progressively to minimise the inevitable squeaking of perished brake blocks. Before setting off, I adjust my scarf, shrug the lumpy canvas rucksack into the centre of my shoulders and adjust my eyes to the dim sodium lighting. To the left is the ever-squeaking extractor fans and droning ductwork of the factory-that-never-sleeps, while to the right lays a journey into a madness that I like and detest in equal measure.

I tip up the right hand pedal with my toe, press down and glide off into the night. It's time to go truck hunting.

The view from the eighth floor.

ACKNOWLEDGEMENTS

Many thanks to Rachel Shepherd for giving me the impetus to write this book. It should have been done via a publishing concern she worked for but that fell through. This left me with little option and the challenge to produce the book myself. Thanks also to my wife Caroline for wading through many film packets and boxes in the home on a daily basis. And to Ian Male and his staff at Walsall College for inspiration.

This book is dedicated to the often un-appreciated hard working drivers who ply their trade day and night, hauling our goods while we sleep. Their long daily hours were eventually rewarded with a good night's rest within the confines of an upholstered steel* box which became their temporary homes.
*or composite in the case of an ERF or Foden!

The photos are best enjoyed in silence. Maybe in a cab with a window slightly ajar to hear the sounds of the night.

This is owner/driver Tommy Snaith's 1974 ERF LV 16-tonner still at work 15 years after manufacture in January 1989. It was parked up for the night in the Perry Barr district of north Birmingham. In the cab can be seen his faithful terrier Trixie. Next day, Tommy would be driving the reliable Gardner powered plodder back up to Richmond in North Yorkshire.

Chapter One

FUMBLING WITH FUNDAMENTALS

I gained an appreciation of photography through the pages of car magazines and was frustrated to have missed it at school. I was dismayed to discover that other lads in my year had been invited to do darkroom work, when I knew nothing about the facility even existing. My Dad had a Kodak Instamatic but it was seldom used with only about three films exposed.

My interest in vehicles stems from seeing them around the working class district of Lozells in Birmingham where I was bought up. Our house was small and crumbly with no bathroom, central heating or garden. The wooden door to the outside toilet had to be kicked in to free it from frost in the winter. The dwelling was eventually condemned. At the back of our house was a yard that had various wooden garages around it and two businesses. One was run by the eccentric Mr Harrison who used to manufacture aluminium pots and pans. He ran battered Morris J Type and Leyland FG vans. Next to that were the premises of the Anthony Brothers who were general mechanics. They had two cars of their own that were fairly uncommon. By the time I was around six years old, I knew both what a Volkswagen Karmann Ghia coupe and a Lancia Flaminia four door saloon looked like, among humdrum Austins.

This photo of a Scania 112m 6x2 tractor with high datum cab was I think taken in 1996. The smart livery was that of Steve Swain Transport of Shrewsbury in Shropshire. Top end Scanias appear in the fleet today and always photograph well.

One evening in early 1988 I met with the driver of a Volvo F7 tractor belonging to P&O and I wondered if I could take some pictures one night down at the container base in Duddeston, central Birmingham. Having been granted permission I took my tripod and made the most of it. Among the trucks on film I got this 1985 MAN 6x2 tractor while behind it lurks a late seventies Seddon Atkinson 400 belonging to FA Nixon of Oldbury in the Black Country.

J. Hayward & Sons of Portland St. Walsall are a local haulier to me, so I naturally have accumulated a few pictures of their lorries over the years. This 1978 ERF B Series 4x2 tractor had done good service for them and it was photographed on a warm night in September 1990. I poked my camera through a wire mesh fence to get a telephoto shot using slow reacting and sharp Kodachrome 25 slide film. Haywards carry mostly steel and concrete products. Today they run a large fleet in a predominantly white livery. Red and brown were the company colours for many years with a change to mid-blue and red in the 1990s.

Creighton ran a fork lift truck hire business and had a depot in the Great Barr district of Birmingham. Photographing their Scania 82m 4x2 tractor in September 1987 was an early subject for my later forays into night time imaging.

Foden Fleetmaster tractors were always a favourite subject of mine to photograph. The Fleetmaster was available in either a composite version or steel S95 cab derivatives like this one. It belonged to Caulkin's Transport of Loggerheads in Market Drayton. They ran at least two of them and were frequent visitors to the Tunnel Cement works in the Digbeth area of central Birmingham. The Foden was captured early one evening in March 1988.

There were no heavier haulage concerns by where we lived. Being a built up area with terraced houses, there wasn't room for transport yards, but further up Lozells Road was a workshop that used to service Regent petrol tankers. These were mostly eight-wheeled Atkinsons as I recall. In nearby Finch road was Collins Express Parcels who ran Ford FK four wheeled box van lorries on parcel duties. These had horrible noisy engines - as if the exhaust system had fallen off. However, many heavy lorries would pass by on the busy Lozells Road and I remember the articulated maroon Foden S34 tippers of Horace Kendrick of Walsall. Mainly because they had the name 'Kendrick' in three-foot high cream painted letters on each tipper body, demonstrating the impact of legible signage.

Among my most pleasant memories as a child were the night walks we went on. Despite living in the heart of an industrial city, in the mid-sixties, my parents would take us three kids on regular Sunday jaunts into the countryside. On summer trips, Dad would go off for a couple of miles as evening became dusk. We'd walk to meet him and I liked it when twilight morphed into darkness. The golden hour, as it is often called. When it snowed, my Mum would take us on treks at night around Handsworth in Birmingham. No-one was around and the atmosphere felt special as the snow glistened under the street lights and fresh drifts creaked under our wellies. I noticed how the shop lights would play on the windows and painted surfaces of the cars. All of this was sinking in.

My fledgling interest in photography had no outlet until the late seventies. My friend David had borrowed a Zenith E camera from his brother in law. We both went to New Street station to expose a roll of 35mm black and white film on trains. I was just a bystander, but took some notice of the process and saw the pictures later. I had little pocket money to speak of, nor was offered any cameras to use, so things stalled. But a desire to take photographs was lingering.

In October 1988 I was experimenting with my Russian Lubitel 6x6 medium format camera. I was learning its limitations and used an F8 aperture and an exposure of just under three minutes to render this Jack Allen bodied Seddon Atkinson 201 refuse collector on film. The Borough of Warrington owned machine would have been in for repair at the Perry Barr, Birmingham Jack Allen works, while parked outside.

I've always thought of the ERF E Series as a modern lorry and in many ways it still is. However when you realise that this photo was taken over 30 years ago in 1988, it dawns on you how much time has elapsed. This pair of Liverpool based E14 twin-steer tractors belonging to Beacon transport were fairly new. The shot required a four minute exposure.

This photograph shows the difficulty of trying to photograph in colour using film under old style street lighting which had a very strong orange cast. The atmosphere is there and the deep blue sky is coming through, but so profound is the amber hue in the artificial light, it's difficult to see what the actual colours of the Scania 111 and Sharples Seddon Atkinson 401 really are.

Just before midnight on the 5th of September 1988, I would have pedalled a couple of miles into the centre of Walsall to J. Hayward and Son. They were the largest local haulage company by me, except for S. Jones who ran many red ERFs in nearby Aldridge. Sharing the Hayward's yard was the small concern of F.E. Clarke who ran both a Leyland Buffalo and a Leyland Marathon in the foreground. Lurking under the glare of a spotlight is the tilted cab of a Hayward Volvo F86 while in the background, parked over the road is a Hayward Volvo F88 ready for work in the next yard.

Barnes and Nelson of Stocks Mill Kendal ran this pair of angular cabbed Volvos. On the left is an F10 registration number PEC 92Y, while on the right is a 6x2 F12 (A901 CEC) which is called Lakeland Rambler. The fleet colours appear to be maroon and grey but the deep amber cast of the street lighting affects the true shades of paint on the cabs. The photograph required a 3 minute exposure at 5.6 and the shot was taken in the early hours of 6th September 1988 in Walsall.

This pair of Bedford KM rigids was employed on scrap metal duties by Charles Dobson. They had a small yard by the Aston Expressway in central Birmingham, a location that is unusual in today's 'urban living' environment where flats and houses are the preferred use. The venerable 1971 example on the left utilised a 6x2 'Chinese six' wheel arrangement with a roll-on/rolloff scrap body while the KM on the right was a more conventional four wheeled skip lorry. The shot was taken in November 1987.

This was a significant image for me since it came out better than expected and convinced me I was on the right track with my night time photography. I was working in a factory on the Tyburn Road in north Birmingham and summoned the energy to explore a few streets in December 1987, taking pictures before heading home on the bus. This Seddon Atkinson 400 tractor was operated by Bardsley's who run a skip hire business and it required a minute to expose the film. They used to run eight wheeled Fodens among smaller 4 wheeled machines. The shot was taken outside haulier Roy S Ely's yard and I was scolded on my return home by my dad since my dinner was burnt. The photo was worth it however!

In 1975 I got my first job as a compliant 16-year old drip, fresh out of school and started work as an apprentice silversmith. Working in a grubby factory was bad enough but I soon realised it was akin to forced labour on the cheap. In reality we 16 year olds 'apprentices' were put on continual production work, doing the same hours as the adults for much less than half the wages. Though initially not as skilled, we nevertheless had to knock out quotas such as soldering hundreds of goblets a day. In the mid-seventies, cameras were in relative terms more expensive than now. Earning around 40 pence per hour was not going to get me a Nikon in a hurry!

I've long had an interest in the sport of drag racing and in 1978 workmate Tony and I got the train to Northampton and then cycled 16 miles to Santa Pod Raceway in Bedfordshire. He lent me a Kodak Instamatic 35mm compact that used 126 sized square format negatives. I excitedly shot my first 24 pictures using the rudimentary point and shoot device. The results were fairly awful, but worse was to follow. Subsequently, I bought my first camera from retailer Dixons. Back then, 110 film was all the rage. This used smaller negatives in a pre-loaded cassette and the salesman persuaded me to part with around 12 quid to buy a small, black plastic abomination, a Kodak 110 Instamatic. Since the negatives were tiny,

Despite having a fairly poor glass, the large negative of my crude Russian Lubitel medium format twin lens reflex camera flattered the lens and gave a usable image. Years later, this shot appeared as a double page spread in Heritage Commercials magazine. The photograph was originally shot in October 1988 and required an exposure of 4 minutes with the lens stopped down to F11 which has rendered movement in the moon and stars. The DAF 3300 belonged to Overland Transport who specialised in Fork lift trucks and the shot was taken outside a crematorium in Great Barr, Birmingham near where I lived at the time.

Whereas around 6 pm in winter is dark, an early autumn night generally has enough light left in the dusky sky. I visited the Blue Circle Cement yard in Handsworth Birmingham to chase the last of the Scammell Routeman tankers they operated and was pleased to capture this 1980 example. The date was Thursday 30th September 1987 and I managed to get a few shots on 50 ISO daylight film, amongst mostly Leyland cement lorries.

the pictures were frankly, dreadful, revealing soft images. I only used about eight films. Years later, I literally threw the camera into the bin with a satisfying 'clang', so no-one else would have to endure such awful shots.

In 1979 I saved up and bought my first 35mm SLR (single lens reflex) camera. A Russian made Zenith TTL. Despite being heavy and crude, it could take good shots in the right hands, though my abilities were limited. I sold it to a friend in 1981 and accumulated enough to buy a Japanese Nikon FM. The Nikon was superbly constructed, simpler to use and mechanically superior. With a 50mm standard lens and accurate light metering, it took excellent photographs from the off. This manual focussing/wind on camera would form the basis of my night time photography.

Sparking my desire to take photographs at night was the American railway photographer Ogle Winston Link. He was featured in the Observer Sunday magazine in the late seventies. I marvelled at the atmosphere conveyed in his shots of steam trains taken in the dark. His personal mission was to record the last days of steam using the Norfolk and Western railroad as his subject before it changed over to diesel locomotives. Link had a background in industrial photography and would meticulously compose each image. To this day, I believe them to be some of the most technically difficult pictures ever recorded on film. He would use miles of cable to direct a series of flashbulbs to discharge simultaneously. He'd one chance at success because he was employing a large format view camera which used a negative some 4x5 inches in size. Just one picture at a time. Needless to say, the quality of the images was astonishing. Check out the photograph *Hotshot Eastbound* from 1956 whereby the entire scene is perfectly exposed. This includes a drive-in theatre with cars and cinema goers in the foreground and a massive locomotive steaming by in the background. This was achieved using a combination of ambient light and flashbulbs and his immense experience. Link had a station wagon and trailer, plus an assistant to set up all his gear. I could never hope to take such a picture, either when I started or even now! However, the atmosphere of a night time image of a truck was something I hoped to emulate in a simpler way - on a push bike.

Chapter 2

MIDNIGHT MAGIRUS

My first attempts at night photography were undertaken over 35 years ago. Unlike today, there was no digital advantage with the scene revealed on the back of a camera screen. There was much guesswork. I took tentative steps using the Nikon FM and a sturdy aluminium tripod to photograph street scenes. I underestimated how dim it was under street lighting but I got my feet wet so to speak, using a couple of seconds exposure on colour print film. Things would later get more involved.

Pioneer had a concrete and cement works in the industrialised district of Duddeston near the city centre of Birmingham, next to the railway line. When my girlfriend (now wife) Caroline knew I was into old lorries, she would occasionally notice anything quirky outside the office where she worked to the north of the city. She mentioned this old split windowed Foden in green. It was noteworthy as its small rounded cab looked rather cute among the large angular modern trucks around it, stood at the traffic lights. When I asked if it had a name on the side she mentioned the word Pioneer. The lorry became known as "Ode Fode" (meaning 'Old Foden' using a bit of Black Country vernacular) and knowing it was local, using the telephone directory, I was determined to track it down. Luckily, the Pioneer plant was not far from the factory where I worked. So one cold night in January 1988, I clocked off work at 5.30 and walked to the establishment. Having secured permission, I took a few pictures with various exposures under the arc lights of this lovely old 1971 Foden S39 cabbed eight legger. It was parked next to a Volvo F7 concrete mixer and I used Fujichrome 50 slide film. At last, 'Ode Fode' was captured for posterity.

■ A fine mean and moody shot from Mark Gredzinski of a pair of Streets' Magirus artics parked for the night in Brum

47

This is the first night time picture I had published. It appeared in the May 1988 issue of Truck and Driver magazine. A pair of Magirus Deutz tractors was indeed a rare sight. They belonged to Streets Transport of Watchet in Somerset. Further details of the photo are in the text.

I remember going to a local park in 1987 and photographing a Bedford TM artic belonging to Danco Marquee Hire of Bristol. The lorry was out in the open under a cloudy night sky. I kept the shutter open for a few seconds on my first shot and then as long as I dared, for half a minute or so. Rather than being anywhere near overexposed as anticipated, the Bedford looked like a muddy box sat in mud. You could hardly make out the lorry. I obviously had much to learn about this night time photography lark, once away from street lighting. Ensuring there would be a lorry to see rather than a murky piece of film indicated that I needed to learn about exposure. Film was hard to come by so it was imperative to make each frame count. Subsequently I visited Birmingham central library and pored over magazines like Amateur Photographer to learn the finer points. Later, when trawling the lorry parks for suitable images, there needed to be pictorial payback for cycling miles and standing around at night. Wasted film and processing was something I literally could not afford. So I read a lot and made notes.

The world is orange

Much town and city lighting, certainly well into the eighties, had a severe colour cast. This proved a challenge. It not only provided poor illumination compared to today's street lighting, but when using colour film it rendered images with a profound orange aura. It was so bad, you could barely tell one colour from another in this sea of deep amber. This was low pressure sodium vapour lighting and was used extensively in Walsall and surrounding areas. Black and white film was unaffected as this was only dependant on monochrome tones. Much as I like B&W, I much prefer colour. (I did take some successful black and white pictures incidentally but chose not to use them for this book).

The early eighties was a time of country-wide recession and I became unemployed after 5 years in the same factory. I received no redundancy pay since the company was liquidated - plus the first couple of years did not count anyway since I was viewed as an apprentice. (Don't just stick the knife in, give it a twist!) This gave

In February 1988 I cycled to central Birmingham to explore the industrial district. It was fairly scary as I recall in dimly lit backstreets but I was keen to get this Magirus Deutz tipper onto the Agfachrome slide film I was using at the time. Doyle Demolition of Dollman Street were the operators and newer Iveco eight leggers can be seen in the background.

me the creative paradox of time to do things, but little money to do them. At the time I was living in the Great Barr district of north Birmingham with my retired Dad. A Polish immigrant (hence my surname), he'd split from my mother around 1974 and she was living in the next town, Walsall. Parsimonious pops took nearly half my dole money as keep, so I had little left over to play with. Arguing over the matter was not recommended.

Generally it's accepted that having limited funds can be a hindrance. The advantage is that it prevents complacency and sharpens the mind to determine how much desire you really have to be creative. I made sure I was up to the task and focussed on what I could actually accomplish with limited resources without the latest photographic trinket.

One Monday night in fair weather, I went out with my tripod and Lubitel to see what was about in the lorry park. This fine lineup of mostly British tackle included a David G. Davies Gardner 320 powered ERF C Series and a pair of Seddon Atkinson 401 tractors. The shot was taken around 3am into Tuesday morning and the 12 minute exposure has left some star trails.

"A hungry hound hunts best"

The quote is one of my favourites from successful veteran American drag racer Don 'Big Daddy' Garlits. He was asked how he managed to finally win a big race that had eluded him in the 1960s. He'd started from the Florida backwaters with nothing and eventually due to hard work and diligence, won hundreds of races and numerous championships over a career that spanned decades. Garlits also built his own cars and was a technical innovator. A memorable image was a dragster at night from the pages of Hot Rod magazine in 1970. It demonstrated the atmospheric possibilities of vehicles at night.

Pursuing time exposures practically meant having a compact photographic setup that could be employed quickly in the field. I could then skedaddle if things got tricky, without the burden of bulky equipment - which I couldn't afford anyway. I discovered that for ten pounds, I could get a shorter, lightweight tripod from Jessops camera store that could be slung in a haversack. It seems strange now, but it took me years to get one since I could never justify that spare tenner. (I remember being down to my last 5 pence one week which was enough to buy a Twix chocolate bar and nothing else.) I owned a decent camera but the hurdle was affording the film. Previously, I had tried transparency or positive film - commonly called slide film. I'd read about Kodachrome and eventually bought a roll. It was often used by professionals, was very stable (I'd read that the colours only *start* to fade after around 100 years) and could be enlarged successfully. Slide film was generally the preferred choice for reproduction in publications, but was notoriously sensitive to underexposure. Kodachrome was process-paid so for around 6 quid, after taking your 36 exposures, mounted slides would be posted to you a week or so later. Its cousin was the cheaper Kodak Ektachrome, but with this, film processing cost extra. Rival companies Fuji and Agfa made similar films. Colour negative print film was fine, but when I tried Kodachrome, I was compelled by its sharpness and depth of colour; but financially, it was out of my league.

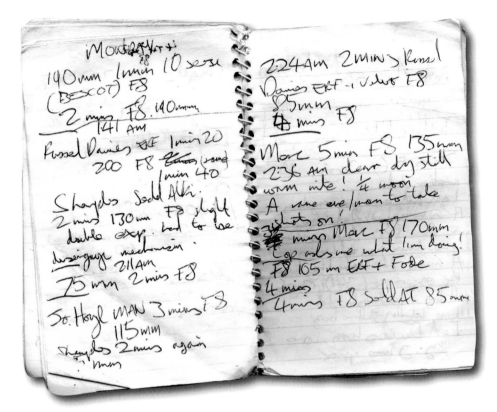

This is two sample pages from the notebook I used to record exposure details in order to obtain consistent results at night. The notes reveal my spidery writing around 1988 I think. Entries in my crude shorthand include 'Russell Davies ERF 1 min 20, 200 F8 (same) 1 min 40.' This meant I took two shots of a Russell Davies tractor at 200mm using my 70 to 210mm zoom lens at an aperture of F8, with the last shot lasting 1 minute 40 seconds. With this I could hopefully remember what the light was like and see which of the two exposures was the more successful. Maybe none were! It was obviously an upbeat night with the entry 'Merc 5 mins F8 135mm. 2.36am quarter moon. A rare eve/morn to take shots on!' The next entry in the sequence reads '3 – half mins Merc, F8 170mm. Cop asks me what I'm doing!' It appeared that I finished photographing that night into morning around 3am.

During a chance visit to a local chemist around 1985, I found some clearance items on the counter. Among them were a few packets of Tudorchrome slide film, which I believe was repackaged from a major manufacturer. It was just £1 per roll. Better still, that included processing and delivery to your door a week later.

This was a common sight in Birmingham back in February 1987. Old buildings were being knocked down in the city centre and this 1982 Ford D Series operated by Ready Mixed Concrete had deposited its load of the wet grey stuff and was ready to leave once the paperwork was sorted. I think the Ford had Perkins V8 power which made a nice noise.

'Cinderella, you *shall* go to the ball!' It wasn't Kodachrome, but was inexpensive and worked. Needless to say, I went back for more and would later visit chemists or camera shops to rummage in the cheap film basket for short-dated film, which was often half-price. Without exception, it always functioned perfectly.

In 1987 I took my first 'serious' night time pictures having secured the lightweight tripod. It was largely made from polycarbonate plastic with skinny, three-section telescoping aluminium legs and was quite flimsy. Once erected, it could hold an SLR camera and small lens. Just.

In early 1988 I decided to go farther afield and cycled to Mum's flat five miles away in Walsall. I chatted to her until the early hours and then pedalled a mile to the back streets of the town centre where I hoped to see a lorry or two. It had been raining and there was no-one around. The quietness was deafening. Shortly, I spotted a pair of seldom seen Magirus Deutz artics parked up under the street lamps. Because it was so eerie, I found getting close to the lorries strangely terrifying and I took just two pictures. One was rather distant but I braved getting closer and filled the frame better with the second shot.

A lorry parked up is a common sight and easily dismissed. However, the public rarely get close up to the massive frontage of a lorry and at night, they become quite intimidating in a way. Especially if you attempt to photograph one without permission of the occupant, slumbering only a few feet away from your lens. It felt as if you were trespassing.

Days later, the film was processed and surprisingly the pictures came out. Flushed with success, I sent the original slide off (like a numpty; it was never returned to me and probably destroyed) and it was published in Truck and Driver magazine in the May 1988 issue. It appeared in the Picture Post column, in which amateur pundits like me could send in pictures of interest to readers. This earned me a welcome ten pounds, which paid for my tripod.

Shattered silence

I found taking pictures of older commercials particularly exciting. Part of my initial remit for taking truck photographs in the first place was to record the last of the British made lorries. These seemed to be diminishing rapidly from our roads and I wanted to capture them on film before they all were gone, as a sort of social document.

Near where I lived in Perry Barr was a royal blue ERF LV. Coming home on the bus I would occasionally pass it parked up in the evening outside the same factory and vowed to photograph it if I saw it again. This characterful 16 ton flatbed four-wheeled rigid was similar to one I'd photographed a year before in Dudley, operated by Penn Transport of Wolverhampton. The LV belonged to Tommy Snaith of Eppleby in Richmond, North Yorkshire. One winter night, I spotted

One of my favourite lorries was the Bedford TM. Especially in its wide cab form as a tractor. By the time I was taking my night shots, these rapidly rusting units were becoming rare, so this was a treat. The subject was Arthur Oakley Transport of Hereford who used to run both ERF C and E Series tractors around the same time and in 2017 took on four new DAF XF tractors, which shows the progression. This unit was Cummins powered making it a lot more economical than the wonderful sounding Detroit Diesel versions. The shot was taken in the early hours of September 1988 and required a 2 minute exposure.

the driver and spoke to him. I enquired about the ERF and found that it was the same one previously in the Penn Transport livery. Tommy had purchased it and decided to go it alone as an owner/driver. I asked if I could take some pictures of it at night and he said sure. I could meet him in the Church Tavern pub around the corner later on. I lived around a mile away, so went home and loaded my Nikon and compact tripod in a haversack.

Tommy and I shared a few pints and got chatting. He told me about how he made it pay driving his old 1973 ERF because it was so economical and other aspects of his hauling life. After 11pm, we walked around the corner back to the lorry and by this time I was feeling the effects of a few pints of bitter. As a bonus, Tommy had a little terrier called Trixie and I managed to take a shot of him with the dog, which would hopefully earn me another tenner in Truck and Driver in the 'Cab Mutt of the month' column. (It did!)

In December 1987 I was walking though some back streets in Birmingham not far from the factory where I worked. With my lightweight and compact tripod wedged in my cheap haversack I was ready for any static lorry pictures that took my fancy. This well used 1977 Seddon Atkinson 400 4x2 tractor with a single-axle low loader trailer fitted the bill. I took a couple of pictures, one of which had some red tail light trails from a passing car across it. The required exposure was two and a half minutes at 5.6 and the lorry belonged to Galvin Civil Engineering.

It was now time to override the alcohol and get some shots of the ERF; I set up the tripod and proceeded to take a few pictures using a cable release. However, being drunk in charge of a camera is neither big nor clever and I caught my foot on one of the spindly tripod legs. Since it was top heavy with the metal bodied camera - over it went. There was a thud and the tinkling sound of smashed glass. Fearing the worst, I retrieved the floppy unit off the hardstanding. Although the camera landed lens first, it was the protective filter that had smashed and not the lens itself. Unfortunately the impact had bent the camera pentaprism and killed the internal light meter. Also the focus on the lens was now rather loose. Since I

was taking future night exposures based on guesswork, this made the half dead but still operable camera ideal for the task as I didn't need an internal light meter. I put the whole incident down to experience, thanked Tommy and stumped home, hoping the pictures would be good enough.

An atmospheric shot was reward enough at the end of a long ride into the night on my bicycle. I would not really entertain this now and it was scary enough back then. It was around four-o-clock in the morning after a still night on 10th September, 1987. I halted at the Tunnel Cement works in the Duddeston area of central Birmingham. This was in the days when such operations could leave their gates open all night. I took a few shots of an ERF B Series eight legger bulk tanker of around 1979 vintage while alongside was an articulated AEC Mandator from 1977, of which Tunnel used to operate a pair. The concern was later renamed Castle Cement, hence the different logo on the door of the AEC. The picture required a 70 second exposure.

In February 1988 I was upstairs on a number 51 bus going from Birmingham to Walsall peering out of the window. While passing the Crest Hotel, I couldn't believe my eyes when I spied this very weird lorry. I quickly jumped off to get a closer look and was rewarded by the sight of a White Streamliner of the later 1940s. Canadian Lager brewer Labatts were attempting to popularise its brand in the UK and used this dramatic articulated dray (of which around ten were made) for publicity. Styled by Russian designer Count Alexis de Sakhnoffsky, the units were ultimately both expensive and impractical. A minutes worth of light on Agfachrome film meant I had a record of the mad device.

Around 1989 when this shot was taken, the new Seddon Atkinson Strato tractors were starting to appear on Britain's roads. I thought it a handsome machine and better looking that the Leyland DAF 95 on which it was based. Douglas Plant had a depot near me in Perry Barr Birmingham and I think this was the first Strato I ever saw. Using my Russian Lubitel 6x6 camera and a couple of minutes exposure I captured the lorry for posterity. Thirty years later, they still look fresh.

Later that year I made the first of a few forays around the back streets and lorry parks of Walsall. I'd chat with Mater till past midnight, and following a check of the watch, I was off on my bike. I used whatever film I had in the camera and although I got some reasonable shots, it was rather hit and miss, with exposures that took minutes rather than seconds in the dim lighting. Thankfully there were enough ERF and Seddon Atkinson lorries parked up, together with Scania 111s etc., which were my kind of subject.

After a few trips, I found getting decent colour pictures so frustrating that my early adventures to the lorry parks petered out. There was too much effort required to just get a lot of orange tinged photographs. I also had other things to occupy

In the Vauxhall district of central Birmingham are a lot of industrial premises and among them was John Smith Wire. They were using this 1986 Leyland Freighter 16 ton dropside lorry to carry their coiled drawn steel wire products. I was passing by their premises which had the shutter door open and got the shot, hand-held on the ground in February 1988.

myself that didn't put the fear of God up me; or tire me out getting home at 4am after an eight mile trip, hunched over a bicycle with a metal camera digging into my back. That said, I did get some gems and if I knew then what I know now……………

All apertures great and small

The following may be of some interest to those not familiar with the technical aspects of conventional film photography. It might help explain some of the difficulties of taking pictures at night.

The aperture in a camera lens works in the same way as the iris in the pupil of a human eye. The thin metal iris or aperture within a lens can go from a small hole to restrict light reaching the film (the lens is then said to be 'stopped down') or the aperture is made larger and is said to be 'wide open.' The co-relation between the aperture through which the light passes and the fractions of a second between the shutter curtains determines how much light reaches the film. An internal light meter indicates whether the combination of the two factors will yield a 'correct' exposure via a needle or LED lights in the viewfinder. The controls are adjusted accordingly in a manually operated camera.

Film exposures in daylight are generally in fractions of a second. For example, photographing a truck using colour film at 100 ISO sensitivity, would require a shutter speed of around 500th of a second on a bright cloudy day using an aperture of F5.6. (the seemingly arbitrary numbers of F2, F4, 5.6, F8 etc are just a sequence of 'click stops' expressed as fractions. The numbers could as well be 1,2,3,4 or A,B,C,D, etc, but that's the way it is in photographic terms….) The higher the number, the smaller the aperture hole gets. 5.6 for example lets in half as much light as F4. This sounds contradictory I realise.

Sometime in the late 1980s I was mooching around central Birmingham looking for pictures. I spied this Bedford KM 16-tonner under the arches in the Digbeth area of the city and thought it might make a good subject. Some passing car headlamps added a bit of drama during an exposure that lasted a couple of minutes.

On the same night the Pioneer Foden was photographed, I saw this tidy 1977 AEC Marshal Major recovery truck run by two friendly guys at their Duddeston garage premises in Birmingham. Having asked permission to take pictures, they obliged by starting her up and putting the lights on which made for some pleasing images. It was after 6pm and I should have been on my way home after a day's production work at a factory, but picture opportunities like this don't happen often.

Meantime a dull cloudy day would require a shutter speed of longer duration at maybe a 30th of a second, using the same aperture of 5.6. This reciprocal would give an accurate 'correct' exposure in both cases. Because the film's sensitivity to light is fixed, the combination of aperture and shutter speed are adjusted to cope with changing light conditions. Automatic exposure systems in modern cameras do all this for you.

Once the sun was going down and twilight conditions commenced, reduced light now required a half to one second exposure. At this slow a shutter speed, there was a risk of camera shake so a tripod or some sort of support for the camera would be essential.

One would presume that in the dead of night the exposures would only be a few seconds more. Often this was not the case due to a phenomenon called reciprocity failure, whereby the formula for shooting in daylight goes out of the window. The exposure in actuality has to be doubled or even quadrupled after a minute or so to get a decent picture without underexposure. Also a condition called colour shift occurs where the dyes in the film emulsion modify and go a bit potty during lengthy exposures. This would normally affect things like portraiture skin tones. The lighting was itself a bit crazy under street lamps, so this didn't really concern me.

Mince pies

Human eyes operate generally in the same way as a fixed focal length camera lens. The process of getting an exposure that is neither too light or dark for our brain to record comfortably is done automatically. Our equivalent of autofocus is the muscles around our eyes and the aperture or iris, is made of soft tissue (rather than thin metal blades in a lens), which go either large or small depending on the amount of light. Think of a cat, with its pupils looking large in the shadows, since the aperture of its iris is wide open. Then if the cat walks into bright sunlight, its iris becomes a slit and its eyeball lens, like in a camera, is similarly 'stopped down'.

Our eyes work well in most conditions, but they are poor in low light compared to many nocturnal animals. Owls for example, have eyes with large lenses that are corrected for low light. This means its eyeball cornea has the ideal shape to be able to focus better within low illumination, gathering the light rays to converge accurately on the back of its eye. Also they have increased amounts of light sensitive receptors to interpret images better in dim conditions than we do. Despite looking intelligent with their big peepers, I was told from an authority on owls that they are in fact, a bit thick! We can perhaps think of a few people like that…..

The most important part of anyone's eye is really the hole in the middle and the shape of the lens which actually focuses the images. The perceived size of the eyes, colour, or the frame of the eyelids is irrelevant to vision quality. Reassuringly there are people with big eyes who are blind as a bat while at the other end are those with small 'piggy' eyes that can see sharp as a tack – and of course, every permutation in between.

Fortunately, taking pictures using long exposures does not require expensive equipment. Specifically, the use of wide aperture lenses, which can be ridiculously pricey. Examples of these are physically long and top heavy lenses used by professionals at things like football matches and indoor sporting events. At such venues, the photographers are not permitted to use flash and light levels can be perilously low. Problems are compounded by the need for high shutter speeds to freeze action.

Before digital, the fastest films were generally 400 ISO (later on, 800 and 1000 ISO emulsions were developed – but were very grainy) and newspaper photographers would mostly use black and white film which was 'push-processed' to compensate. Extra development made the film more sensitive to light. To gather more light on the film (essential at a floodlit football pitch at night), large aperture lenses were developed. Some of these are the size of a KFC Bargain Bucket with large diameter outer lens elements to allow increased levels of light in to reach the film. Furthermore they are optically corrected to work at their best when using wide apertures (rather like an owl's eyes) and the precision grinding, polishing and mounting of this sophisticated optically clear glass is *very* expensive. They are also

exceedingly heavy. They have a specific purpose and many get sold to wealthy amateurs in the belief that it will improve their photography. Ironically, a 70 to 300mm zoom lens can cost just under £100 (I used one for published pictures many times) whereas a typical 300mm 2.8 lens can be over £5000! There are pros and cons in each case, though the former is often more useful on planet real world.

March 1988 saw me in the Duddeston Freightliner depot in central Birmingham. I met up with the driver of a P&O Volvo F7 artic driver whose name I did not record, alas. With his assistance, I gained permission to photograph some lorries at the container base in the early evening. There was still blue in the sky and some 'golden hour' lighting which evaporates as darkness falls. In amongst modern MAN and Volvo FL 7/10 tractors, was this ERF B Series unit. In the background you can see a Scania 111 and both vehicles belonged to local haulier PM Davis whose depot was in nearby Landor Street. Malcolm Davis had a few secondhand Volvo F88 and Scania 111 tractors doing sub-contracting for P&O among others and all were painted in this subtle pale grey colour.

Joint Motorways LTD.
JOINT MOTORWAYS LTD.
JOINT MOTORWAYS LTD.
JM
INTERNATIONAL SERVICES
TEL 0639-884636
FAX 0639-895102
JM52
F732 DCY

Chapter 3

LOITERING AT THE LORRY PARK

My photographic interest was renewed as I noticed that a new type of high pressure sodium lighting was being employed. This offered much better colour rendition. My mother (who'd always encouraged me artistically) pointed out that trucks on the Pleck Road lorry park could now be seen clearly. We passed by in a car one night and I too saw the effect. This gave me the impetus to get going again.

By 1990 I was living in Walsall myself, albeit on the eighth floor of a council tower block. It was only a mile or so to the lorry parks, making access easy. I'd decided to go self-employed as an artist, designer and photographer, despite starting out with no capital or savings whatsoever. I went on the government Enterprise Allowance scheme in which for one year, I'd get 40 pounds a week. It was a way to use my skills so I took a risk and had a go. Having started a family it was worth working from home, where I could look after my young daughter. Flexible hours meant

This Foden 4350 was photographed on Kodachrome 25 ISO film in January 1994. Apparently it was the first truck in the Joint Motorways fleet to have a night heater which would have been very welcome at that time of year in the five year old machine. It served as a demonstrator and was bought new from Fairwood Commercials, Swansea. Carrying a baled load of scrap metal, the 6x4 machine would have pulled well with its 320 Cummins and 13 speed Fuller 'box.

This depicts a 1993 Foden 4350 tractor in a 6x2 configuration belonging to Charlson who seemed to specialise in container transport. The Foden 4000 Series used the Mk4 version of the S10 cab and was a worthwhile development in the Foden line. Despite not using the traditional Foden script on the cab front, it can be seen on the rubber moulding above the front step. I was always mystified as to why Foden did not pick this out in white by way of branding. Anyway, the shot was taken around 1995 on a wet night after the rain had stopped.

that if I went out in the early hours and returned at three am, I didn't have to get up at 6.30 to work in a factory as before. I realise that this is a lie-in for truckers (!) but it's hard to function properly on little sleep. So I got going again. Only this time, I tried to be little more organised.

To ensure repeatability, I would keep the aperture of the lens always at 5.6 with few exceptions. This meant that there would be enough in focus on an articulated unit from cab front to the end of the trailer. Generally, the more a lens is stopped down, the deeper the depth of focus. The opposite is true the other way round and a large aperture like F2.8 will result in a shallower depth of field (an advantage in things like portraiture as a defocussed background can be more pleasing). Secondly, the hole in the iris at 5.6 let in enough light so I would be standing around most times for seconds, rather than minutes when a truck was directly under street lamps. However, in the gloom of an unlit back street, exposures of four minutes or so were unavoidable. Thirdly, 5.6 to the next click stop down was generally the sweet spot, which technically resulted in the lens recording its sharpest images.

When funds allowed, I would use the sharpest film, which was generally the slowest to react to light. Since I was using a tripod for long exposures, this didn't matter and I'd be rewarded with grain-free images. The films used were mostly Kodachrome 64, Ektachome 64T or Fujichrome 64T. The key numbers were 64 which referred to the ISO sensitivity of the film. The 'T' meant 'tungsten balanced'.

Most colour film is 'daylight balanced' which means that it's formulated to react to a colour temperature higher than 3200 degrees. Colour temperature is measured in degrees Kelvin. Daylight film is generally set at 5600 degrees which is around the bluey white light we perceive outdoors. When the redder, lower temperature, side of the spectrum like incandescent lighting is encountered, daylight film renders this yellow to orange. Tungsten film is designed for these conditions, whereby the film emulsion dyes are formulated to negate most of the reddish hues into blue, rendering colours more like daylight. However, should you use tungsten balanced

Based in Gloucester, RF Horsman was Rex Horsman an owner operator I believe, trading as Transrex. I spoke to him as he parked up one warm evening in July 1993 at a Walsall lorry park and he was happy for me to take some shots. I returned a while later as the curtains were closed to get this image in the twilight. His 1985 ERF C Series was replaced by an equally clean ERF EC14 tractor.

McCall Bros of Glasgow have had a long history of Scania usage for their heavy haulage work over the years. I had seen these Scanias before, a 112 on the left and this 1992 143H (for heavy duty) V8 tractor. Both were carrying steel, slightly rusted pipes on extendable trailers. I remember talking to one of the drivers as he parked up one evening. I recall he was a nice guy and even wanted to buy a picture from me. There's a rarity! June 1993 was the date and I was using a moderately wideangle 28mm lens on a second hand Olympus OM 1 camera I'd just bought.

From Saundersfoot in Dyfed, GA Rossiter Traction Services (more interesting than just 'haulage') were the owners of this ERF B Series six wheeled tractor. In June 1992, this type of lorry was increasingly becoming a rare sight. The registration number was GTW 901W, making this particular ERF around 1981 vintage.

film in daylight, all your pictures will have an unpleasant blue cast. Tungsten balanced film incidentally, was often used deliberately in cinema applications, to create an artificial night time scenario.

Digital cameras have settings to compensate for this, called the 'white balance.' An automatic white balance in the camera will give naturalistic images under most lighting conditions. We humans have an automatic white balance, and it's called the brain. This means we don't observe, the rather green cast in actuality under fluorescent lighting for example. Or notice just how phenomenally amber it is in reality around conventional light bulbs.

Another way to compensate for the orange cast of daylight film at night is the use of blue filters. I'd tried these with some success. However, they absorb much of the light and in some cases the exposure had to be doubled or tripled again, which was tiresome. So Tungsten balanced film was the way to go.

Time management

I reasoned that if I kept the film speed and the aperture on the lens the same, the only variable would be the amount of time the shutter would be open. Interpreting how much light there was around in a given environment would achieve better exposures. To assist matters, I took along a small notebook and pen to record the subject and relevant exposure times. I was pretty diligent and for a few years, I'd scribble down details next to the trucks. Sometimes it was done from memory and written up later. Often it was too cold to take off my gloves to fumble for the pages. I developed my own form of shorthand which would mention the

Laden with pipes, this 1990 Seddon Atkinson Strato 6x2 tractor had its wheels tuned at a jaunty angle as it reverse parked one night in September 1994. I was using Kodachrome 64 daylight balanced slide film and the truck was operated by Wavin Industrial Products Limited of Durham who make polyethylene and PVC pipework.

Around 1990, a typical visitor to the backstreets of Walsall and the lorry parks was this 1988 MAN F90 4x2 tractor with tri-axle curtainside trailer. One of many Cumbrian visitors, Barnett and Graham Ltd from Penrith used to run MANs into double figures on Bulk work. You can see the flare from the street lamp on the top left starting to creep into the picture and this was something you had to keep a close eye on when looking through the camera viewfinder, particularly if using a wideangle lens like this. Sometimes it would add to the atmosphere of the shot and the orange cast compliments the blueness of the sky effectively atop the damp road surface. Due to the colour casts, it may be hard to tell that the tractor and trailer are predominantly green in hue.

This is my yellow 1975 Sun steel framed bike parked up at the lorry park in front of the police station. Most of my pictures were taken using the Sun and I still have it. Since I dislike dropped handlebars, I now ride it more upright with swept back 'North Road' bars and it performs better than ever, despite its age. It was literally a clear moonlit light when I captured this 1988 Mercedes SK and van bodied trailer on film. The operator was ER Miles and Sons of Cymmer, South Wales.

A summer night with a gentle breeze got the poplar trees swaying during a long exposure around 1994. On the left was a big new Mercedes Powerliner V8 run by Rawlings Transport of Hook in Hampshire who had been in business since 1972. They still run Mercedes trucks. To the right was a smaller 1985 Volvo F7 belonging to C, Butt of Northampton who nowadays also run Mercedes vehicles.

Based in Stalybridge, Cheshire, Bay Freight were established in 1960 and nowadays their livery is blue and white with red trim. DAF XF tractors have featured in the fleet of late. Back in November 1990, Bay Freight had a number of Seddon Atkinson tractors on the books in this largely pale green hue, although it's hard to tell under the street lamps employed around November 1990. This photo of their 1985 301 tractor took about three minutes to record onto film.

One winter morning in the early 90s found this Mercedes SK and unusual trailer parked up. It was literally a boat load and the appropriately name Sealand Boat Deliveries Ltd were performing the task. Boats are bulky but relatively light when they are this size and Lancashire based Sealand have been hauling them for over 40 years. DAF XF tractors feature in the fleet nowadays.

Late summer into autumn months mean a longer twilight into darkness period than winter. This shot of a Canning of Leyland Volvo FL 10 illustrates this. Canning used to run Atkinson Borderer and AEC tractors. Later in the 1980s Leyland Roadtrains and Seddon Atkinsons figured in the fleet. A Monday evening in early September 1990 found the nearly new Volvo looking immaculate under the street lamps.

specific truck or, if it was new to me, might be something general like 'blue Foden, Doncaster, 90 seconds, top lorry park' to remind me later. After a few years, I got so used to assessing lighting conditions, I could dispense with writing notes and take pictures relying solely on experience.

Night jitters

Did I mention I was scared? Well I was. Often. Naturally the fear was of my own making. Dread of the unknown, magnified by imagination. Had I known nothing untoward would happen I could have photographed with a relaxed impunity. But sometimes you need a nervous dynamic even in a benign endeavour like taking pictures, to give you an edge and literally look sharp.

Often I would take a packet of cigarettes out with me. As an occasional smoker I'm not nicotine dependant, but I'd enjoy lighting up a Camel both to kill time and give myself something to do at 3am and calm my nerves! I'd light up a fag as a reward for having got through the scary bit, which was mostly the back streets. "What am I doing here?" is something I would say to myself repeatedly - in between inevitable mumblings and expletives. Talking to yourself for reassurance helped diminish the pant-soiling factor. When I questioned my motives or doubted the worth of the photography, the answer would arrive a couple of weeks later. Among occasional disappointments were pictures that made you go "wow"! When pictorial expectations were exceeded, it definitely became worthwhile.

Of the many types of lorry that I like to photograph, I have to say that in general, Fodens are among my favourite. I just think they have bags of character and I think this 1987 Foden S10 cab Mk3 tractor proves the point. This S106 was a 6x4 double drive unit which was championed by PACCAR, the American owners of Foden at the time and this split window machine does have that USA look to it. Wolfendale Brothers Ltd of Salford were the operators and the rig, complete with Boalloy Tautliner trailer, was photographed in the early hours around 1992.

There are some wonderful liveries on many Scottish trucks and the ERFs of JB McBean are a fine example of this. From East Calder in West Lothian, McBean have always had a buy British policy with their Lorries with Fodens and Scammell Crusaders appearing in the past. This 1990 ERF E14 heavy haulage tractor with an extendable trailer was one of many ERFs on the books and an eight legger ERF C Series was another noteworthy machine I used to see at the lorry park. The shot was taken around 1994.

A rare visitor in August 1989 would have been this Spanish derived Dodge 300 Series, a model which lasted from 1972 to 1982. This 1980 example belonged to Burgoynes of Lyonshall in Herefordshire. They used to run at least nine of these lorries and it took over three minutes to record it on film.

GCS Johnson of Richmond in North Yorks specialise in heavy haulage and this 1990 Leyland DAF 95 could weigh up to 80 tonnes including the unit and trailer. It was making light work of the JCB on the back when this photo was taken in January 1994. Behind was a 1988 ERF E Series owned by Walpole and Wright whose lorries were regular visitors to the park. The large poster hoarding at the back is not illuminated. When it was, the lighting played over the Scania 113 on the cover shot of Midnight Movers.

This yellow Mercedes Actros 2535 appears to my eyes to have more of an acid yellow hue than the warmer tones that appear in daylight. This was because of the more blue aspect of the tungsten balanced film used and the ambient artificial lighting itself. The 1998 6x2 tractor was photographed when pretty new and was one of the large clean fleet belonging to P&O Ferrymasters.

I took this shot in January 1992 and decided to scan the piece of film in its entirety so the reader can see exactly what I saw in the viewfinder at the time. This handsome Seddon Atkinson Strato was no more than a year old and was run by JD Crawford & Co. of Haltwhistle in Northumberland. I opened up the aperture to F4 making the exposure relatively brief at about a minute. I must have been cold and wanted to get back quickly. It was half past three in the morning!

This was a typical scene at the lorry park in 1988. Under the yellow cast of the street lighting can be seen various tractors including a 1982 Hills of Cardiff Seddon Atkinson 400, Pritchards of Pontypool DAF 2100 and a Sharples of Preston Seddon Atkinson 401. Looking at the star trails, it would have been a few minutes to record this lot on film.

Around the summer of 1990, I was using an ancient Halina twin-lens reflex given to me by my mother in law. I agreed to try it out. I knew the lens would be average at best so decided to use a small aperture of F11 which would give enough depth of focus and adequate sharpness to prevent the exercise being a waste of time. Because of this, the exposures would be longer than usual. I put the camera on the ground and hoped for the best. This characterful 1986 DAF 3300 Space Cab 38 tonner belonging to Ian Catt of Preston was the subject. It took around sixteen and a half minutes to record the lorry on film and I finished at 3.30 in the morning.

I didn't really talk about my exploits. Most people had little interest or understanding. If anything, they shed pity on my little obsession. I accepted that no-one would share my fascination, but I reasoned that if I kept the quality of the images high, *one day*, this might mean something as a body of work. I was under no illusions that I was creating high art and most pictures were mere record shots. Trucks at night? So flippin' what, yer David Bailey wannabe! However, there was no denying that even with a cynical, self-critical head, some of the photographs were exceptional. And who else had them? What other chump was daft enough to venture out in the desperate early hours in an industrial town, unpaid, for documentary photographs that no-one cared about? *One day......*

Any conversations I had with drivers at night were few and far between. They tended to be in the twilight hours of summer if I headed out for some early evening shots. I'd explain what I was doing and ask; did they mind if I took a few pictures? In every case I had permission with no problem. Most drivers could not really understand my interest and shrugged their shoulders in a 'whatever floats your boat' kind of way. Some asked a few questions and I did explain to legitimise my request, that at some point I wanted to produce a book. Ultimately, I had every intention of doing so. Or was I just convincing myself? With empty pockets, I had no inkling of realistically how it could happen. But dwelling on impossibilities was pointless. Unless I could produce decent pictures reliably, a book would *never* proceed, with or without a publisher. So I carried on. I met some nice guys along the way and it was always a pleasure.

It was early September in 1988 when I captured this Scania 141 tucked away in a corner near a factory in Walsall. It belonged to Andy Aplin Transport and had quite a bit of attention paid to the look of the machine to make it stand out as a custom device. Three minutes at F5.6 was adequate time for a successful exposure in the shadows.

So dim was the illumination at the back of the lorry park, the light from the cab of this 1985 ERF C Series drawbar rig has thrown down a bright pool as the driver relaxed in his cab. It was beyond midnight and I'm thinking the shot was taken around 1990. It required about three minutes rendering the Myers Beds machine onto film.

This shot was one of a series of experiments I did using two exposures on the same piece of film. When it worked it was effective. The idea was to render a clear, big moon on a dark sky. Firstly, using a tripod and a 400mm Tokina telephoto lens, I shot an entire roll of 36 exposure tungsten balanced slide film of the moon itself. I had the camera set up on the balcony of the flat where I lived and I was careful to keep the moon in the centre of the frame, always towards the top of the sky. Then I'd rewind the film into its canister, slowing down at the end to make sure that the flappy bit at the end (the film leader) was not rewound into the cassette. I would then open the camera back, re-load the film again, wind on and utilise a shorter 50mm 'standard' lens that I used for most of my trucks at night shots.

On the next clear night, I'd go out as usual but on each shot I set the truck subject deliberately low in the frame, leaving as much sky in the frame as possible. This would install a big spectacular moon in the night sky. Sometimes the moon would encroach across a random chimney or the top of the truck cab itself, so it was a bit hit and miss. On this picture, taken in February 1995 at around 3am, the moon (which does not exist right now in reality) is hovering over the main police station in Walsall. On the left is a 1992 Cardiff Transport ERF E Series powered by a Perkins TX 400bhp diesel while on the right is a Van Hool chemical tanker belonging to Fern, hauled by a 1987 MAN 16-331. Cardiff Transport used to haul steel from South Wales to Scotland in a day if possible. I stood for a minute or so as the mechanical Pentax MX camera took the picture. As this is written, the police station is demolished, the lorry park had been built upon and more than likely, both trucks have been scrapped. It's a reminder that the commonplace does not last forever.

37

There were not always that many trucks in the secure lorry park and sometimes the gate was locked. On this occasion, around 1990, there was a Scania 111 that was a definite candidate to record on film. Run by Scotts Heavy Haulage of Ireland but based in Alfreton in Derbyshire, this 1980 unit was parked alongside a much newer Volvo FL10 belonging to John Raymond of South Wales.

"You've got to have a system"

As Harry Hill would say. Although I was gradually losing my fear of going out at night, there were always moments when you were on edge. And at times it was deeply unpleasant. It was never an entirely comfortable experience, even on glorious summer nights when the air was warm. Just me, sharing the pavement and gutters with the occasional resentful rodent.

Parading around the lorry parks and streets was something of a lottery. At first I was a bit random in my approach but eventually got into a rhythm, to start and finish the photo session in much the same way. This avoided hanging around. One variable was the choice of lorries. Sometimes there were lean pickings. Either the same lorry you saw last time or few subjects worth photographing. Conversely, some nights had a bonanza of interesting machines to the point where it was dismaying to know that it would be at least three hours work to try and do everything justice. At 3am, after intense concentration and dry stinging eyes, you felt dead on your feet. I was desperate to go home and crawl into bed……. but there was one lorry park to go and you had to get that old Foden you spotted earlier, plus that immaculate sign-written ERF and….

Sometimes, I had to literally get on my hands and knees, getting the subject correctly in the tiny viewfinder to avoid lopping the back off the trailer or cab roof. Flare from street lights sprayed across the lens when a lorry was backlit. Sometimes you'd use one hand as a makeshift lens hood and have it hovering somewhere between the lens and the street lamp to negate flare. I should point out to any photographers that I actually used proprietary lens hoods, which are recommended. But since only source of main lighting was from the councils' finest, things didn't always work out like in camera magazines. You literally had to think on your feet. Or gravel encrusted wet knees in my case.

December 1991 saw a dry, still night which was ideal for taking pictures in the early hours. A 1983 Bedford TM tractor was a rare treat to capture on film. I had seen them before but only in daytime, operated by Cormar Carpets of Bury in Greater Manchester. They had been in the carpet trade since the 1920s and used to major on Bedford TKs. Cormar additionally had some Bedford TM 16 tonners too.

Though most pictures had the subject as a static vehicle at night, this was a case where I had set up the tripod to record the vehicle both stationary and then having it move to render it semi-blurred. The camera was set up deliberately to do this and hit the shutter at the appropriate time. A Syd Wood of Rotherham Iveco 38-ton tractor was picking up and dropping off trailers in the secure lorry park.

With better ambient street lighting and the use of Tungsten balanced film, much of the amber cast is gone from my later shots. This gave the lorries a more naturalistic feel, as if in daylight. This 1985 Seddon Atkinson 401 carries plenty of road dust up its flanks and was a fine looking working machine with its tri-axle tipper. J&M Collinson Ltd of Garstang in Lancs was the operator and the shot was taken around September 1994.

Chapter 4

RING THE CAVALRY

Most times a photo session at Walsall's lorry parks and streets was uneventful. Save for the inevitable cold, fear and dread. I'd already encountered the police years before. They would often spot me at night, driving by slowly to check what I was up to. One night I'd been approached by a friendly pair of coppers in a squad car in the early hours. They pulled up slowly behind me at a lorry park, which was conveniently in front of the main police station. I felt relatively safe there. A lady officer wound her window down and asked cheerily. "Hello, can I ask what you are taking photographs for? We've seen you around a few times and wondered what you are doing"

I replied "I like taking photographs of lorries. It's just a hobby of mine". She smiled with a quizzical look "Bit of a strange hobby isn't it? Why are you taking

Car transporters parked up at night were not that common but one firm was a regular visitor at night and the lorries of ECM of Carlisle very often would turn up in pairs. This 1991 Mercedes Powerliner was ahead of an older model Merc and appears to have Toyota vehicles on board in March 1995.

41

It would have taken over a minute to record this handsome pair on film. On the left is a 1989 Mercedes Powerliner 2 belonging to Bradbury's Ltd of Cheadle in Staffs. 'Rambo' would have neatly roped and sheeted his load whereas the driver of the William Armstrong of Longtown machine arguably had an easier task with the curtainside trailer on his fairly new Scania 113m. A clear June night in 1992 saw me fire one shot with flash on the right during the exposure, to brighten some of the shadows.

Robbins of Swansea used to run Scammell Crusaders, ERFS and Fodens. Nice Tackle! Here's a less glamorous but worthy Leyland Cruiser which was parked up with a load of cable drums on board, parked in a Walsall back street. There's a thin layer of frost underfoot and it would have been around a four minute exposure to get the shot right, sometime in the early 1990s.

It was turning dusk as the last light of the sky picked out the shiny contours of this new and exceptionally smart ERF E Series. David G Davies of Glossop in Derbyshire had run Seddons and ERF B Series in the past. I used a 19mm ultra wideangle lens for this shot to record K3 DGD on Agfachrome 100. I used a low angle which exaggerated the inherent distortion within the lens. Also, by putting the camera on the ground I could use a one second exposure without camera shake, since I was not using a tripod that evening in July 1993.

A Kenworth in Walsall! This was a frantic grab shot as I attempted to erect my tripod in record time before the truck fled. This was a night in May 1990 and I'd just started my 'shift' and was cycling in front of the main police station on my way to the lorry parks. This dazzling circa 1979 Kenworth K100 cabover possibly had its driver asking for directions. Either way, it was about to go and I could not get the haversack off my back quick enough to take a shot of this rare visitor.

This chained load of steel pipes on the flatbed trailer was pulled by a 1988 6x2 Volvo FL10. The operator was A&W Fullarton of Govan Road Glasgow, but the dominant orange hue of the street lighting has made the cab colour hard to decipher. The shot was taken around 1992 I would think and the exposure of around three minutes has caught the sway in the background tree leaves.

I managed to get a few Millicans lorries on film and they were something of a mystery at night as I seldom saw them in the daytime. Jos Millican of Longtown in Cumbria ran many an ERF and this planked timber load was typical. This 1989 E14 was taken in January 1992 and would have absconded from the Walsall car park just a few hours later.

This ERF EC12 was only around a year old and made a wonderful sight in March 1999. Some sort of corrosive liquid was in the tri-axle tanker and William Blyth of Church, Accrington has been producing chemicals since 1845. To ensure maximum sharpness I stopped the lens down on my Pentax MX to F8 and took a few shots to get this photo correctly exposed onto film.

It was rare to see an eight wheeled tipper like this tautly sheeted ERF E10 example as they mostly work days. However it's not all muck shifting and scrap on local work and Rufford of Knutsford supplied top dressing for sports turf on things like golf courses. Their services would go country wide, hence this ERF parked up in Walsall in March 1995.

If you look above the robust Lawsons of Cockermouth Scania 112m, you can see the partial eclipse of the moon. I had taken a series of shots earlier using a 400mm telephoto lens from the balcony of the flats where I lived in a technique explained earlier. The film was then rewound in the camera and now using a shorter 50mm lens, I shot the film again, trying to keep the previous weird dark moon image always in the top of the frame. It didn't always work, but then I expected a few failures. On the first of April 1999 I was the only fool standing around at the top of Long Street at 2am, taking pictures of a big lorry with a pipe load.

them at night?" I explained that I was attempting to capture the atmosphere and lighting effects of the vehicles and the reason I was out in the early hours was not to be disturbed or attract attention from anyone. I'd been taking pictures for years and lived locally. My name and address didn't elicit a murmur on the police computer. (Unless it flagged up previous convictions of being a dullard in charge of a camera. Despite being a repeat offender, there was no law against that yet). Having ascertained I was no threat to the public, they cruised off into the night, probably having a justifiable chuckle.

There were lengthy gaps in my night time photographic capers. I wasn't approached again and the incident must have been forgotten about by the feds. However, one memorable night years later turned out to be like something out of a movie.

I'm unsure of the exact date, but it was early into a photo session, just before 1am. I was standing on the pavement by the corner of Brook Street and the expanse of Long Street. The latter runs parallel to the railway line near Walsall station, where many trucks would park up. I'd often start my night's work here and it's still popular with overnight truckers now. A few may read this and check the street signs to see where I mean. The tripod was at

Flare from street lighting can be the night time photographer's enemy, but here it has worked a little artistic magic in the background. The subject was a 1985 JH Myers of Clitheroe Lancs, ERF C Series CP turbo pulling a tri-axle tipper. John Myers had a buy British policy at the time and ran some B Series ERFs too. March 1995 meant around 10 years of hard use had passed under the wheels of the unit and it would have taken around 25 seconds to record the characterful ERF on film.

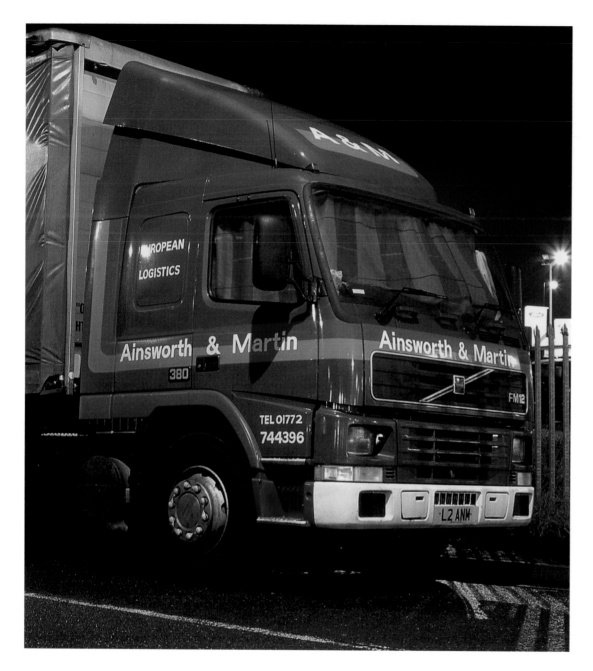

It was June 1992 when this Volvo Globetrotter was seen. Parked next to the Smiths flour mill, the driver of F496 YFY of was assured of a good night's sleep in the confines of the spacious Volvo F12 cab with its extra headroom. The tanker was operated by James Lynch of Sandbach who still use FH12 Globetrotters on acid and alkali tanker work.

This was a relatively recent picture, taken in December 2006. I was experimenting with an inexpensive polycarbonate bodied Canon T60 and a 50mm standard lens to see how it performed. The subject was a Volvo FM12 6x2 tractor and the Ainsworth and Martin of Preston livery had decent colour on it. It was parked near a Galvanising plant in Walsall that ran a night shift, so I felt relatively safe.

Not every truck parked up at night was a 38 ton heavy tractor and these two relative lightweights are proof of that. It was a summer night around 1990 when I spied these two fairly new Leyland Roadrunners belonging to Forster's of Sandysike, Longtown in Cumbria. The exposure was four minutes at F11 on my Lubitel and the shot was taken around 1am on a session starting on a Monday night into early hours of a Tuesday morning.

An overnight Castrol tanker was fairly unusual and this 1989 Volvo FL10 was loaded with mineral oils for industrial use one suspects. The shot was taken in early January 1992 and despite using the Fuji 64 ISO tungsten balanced film I had recently acquired, it has struggled to render the green and red Castrol bands accurately, such was the strength of the orangey Sodium lighting.

A popular parking up spot was the short street by the side of Smiths Flour Mill in Walsall. In September 1990 it was very much in operation, whereas now it has been converted into dwellings. On the right of the shot can be seen two tri-axle articulated bulkers belonging to Banks Grain. The main subject is a 1983 DAF 2500 operated by H. Morgan and Sons of Cwm who still run a tidy fleet of green DAFs among others. Largely on steel haulage, being as it was early evening I would have asked permission from both drivers to take pictures. Behind was F661 BTH, a Caterpillar powered Foden 4300.

maximum extension and I was standing upright composing in the viewfinder to fill the frame, when I heard a cacophony of police sirens in the distance. 'Something's up' I thought, but reassured myself that it had nothing to do with me and carried on.

Prior to this I had taken a couple of pictures in the secure lorry park at the top of Brook Street. By now into my stride with a reliable system of working, I felt more confident at night. However, setting up the tripod and taking it down when moving to a new location was always a fiddly chore, making sure each leg was locked/ unlocked properly. The secure lorry park was at the crest of a short incline. Rather than undo the nine locks within the three tripod legs, to save time I'd pull the legs together, still with camera attached and stuff the whole thing under my arm. I'd mount my bicycle and simply coast the 100 feet downhill, traversing the crossroads of Queen Street (checking for traffic left and right) onto Long Street, braking with my free hand. I had my balaclava on to keep out the cold and the tripod tucked under my armpit with its legs sticking out. It was innocent enough…..except to one man watching at a window….

Meanwhile, back on Long Street, I got the lens focussed and became aware of high revving engines. Taking my eye away from the viewfinder, I observed flying up Bridgeman Street to my left, three police cars with flashing blue lights, but no sirens. A couple of minutes later, two more flew by. 'Obviously a major incident' I thought to myself and was glad it's all well past me. Continuing with my photography, I'm soon in my own quiet world again. ' tilt the tripod head

This was a chance shot in a way. Around November 2011, I was on a college course studying Photography in Walsall. Everyone on the course was engaged in taking night pictures as part of the curriculum on this particular early evening and pretty soon I wandered off by myself to see if there was any night time activity at nearby Haywards' yard. Old habits die hard. Sure enough, there was a Mercedes Actros parked up. Using a digital Nikon D3100 borrowed from college and just a standard kit lens 18-55 zoom I was able get the truck with a 13 second exposure and had the luxury of looking at the rear screen to see if the shot came out.

Around 1992 the early hours would see a pair of Iveco 220-36 38 ton tractors doing a regular trailer swap at the Walsall secure lorry park. On a summer night, when the windows were open on the eighth floor of the tower block where I lived, you could hear them going about their business. Syd Wood of Tenter Street, Rotherham were the operators, with steel bar the load. I selected this image to show the ghost image of the driver winding the trailer legs in position.

This photograph was taken some 30 years ago which is somewhat shocking. It shows a typical lorry park scene of the time with a Caswell of Abergavenny Seddon Atkinson 301 in the foreground and ERF C Series tractors belonging to Prestons of Potto and James Nuttall respectively. It almost looks like a summer evening but in reality, the gloomy shadows of a November 1990 night at 1am required the camera shutter to be open for six and a half minutes, using a 28mm wideangle lens.

It would take the certainty of a warm June night in 1995 to allow this big load of hay bales to be transported without any kind of sheeting for the overnight stop. LE Jones of Ruthin has always had a nice livery and smart Scanias still dominate the North Wales fleet. Specialising in Livestock transport, this late Scania 113m tractor was taken on daylight Kodachrome 64 ISO film and the sharp Carl Zeiss lens of my favourite camera at the time, a Contax 159, rendered the truck faithfully.

Light rain earlier in the evening was still evident in the rivulets streaming down the cab mounted airfoil of this late model Leyland Roadtrain 20-33 6x2 tractor. Naylor's Transport of Leyland, Lancs used to have a Leyland Marathon tractor that would park in the same place in Walsall some years earlier but I never got a night shot of it. This handsome short wheelbase tractor has always been a favourite of mine and the chassis has Scammell Trunker origins from the sixties. This unit had a 325 turbo intercooled diesel and J781 JCW had a number plate in the screen that read 'Steve' which should identify the driver.

up a little, check the focus, aperture ring hasn't moved…' when immediately the volume goes up and I'm aware of rapidly encroaching, increasingly loud engines, blazing headlights and flashing blues coming from the left, the right and directly behind me. Swiftly, I realise that I might be the cause of the pandemonium. I reason that although the world has suddenly gone rather mad, I'm not doing anything wrong. So I literally stand my ground. It occurred that figuratively speaking, I must look like a rabbit in the headlights - or at least one holding a

cable release in its right paw. I was illuminated by at least six pairs of Lucas' finest full-beams and one copper literally drove up the pavement and stopped a couple of feet to the left of me, Starsky and Hutch style. While bombarded with the sound of slamming doors above blinding lights, two thoughts occurred; Firstly, I was impressed with the co-ordinated pincer movement, with the initial cars sighting me as their quarry earlier, then organising the rest to converge simultaneously. I anticipated brisk questioning coming in a second. But secondly, my overriding

Truswell Haulage of Sheffield often used to drop off and pick up trailers in the early hours, as with this scene from June 1992. The load in this case was coiled steel wire and a pair of Scania 113m tractors with low datum cabs were on the job. I liked the composition of the shot with the two open doors while the driver attended to the trailer legs. Fortunately the main headlight beams were not on or else the resultant flare on the lens would have spoiled the shot.

From Swansea came the fleet of Geo. Beer which mainly centred on British tackle that included ERF, Seddon Atkinson and Fodens like this red beauty. The subject was a steel cabbed Foden S95 Fleetmaster and it was photographed with a partial load in January 1992. To save time I opened up the aperture of the lens to F4 which reduced the exposure time to one minute and used two open flashes to hopefully illuminate the shadows on the side of the trailer. Thankfully, it came out as envisaged.

thought was 'Don't wake the driver!' I figured that whatever this was about would soon be resolved - but don't disturb the poor trucker from his slumber. However, something told me not to make any sudden movements......

The interrogation started; "What are you doing?" barked the senior officer. "I'm taking photographs....." I replied, stating the bleedin' obvious "...of trucks at night."   I'm illuminated like Blackpool Tower by police headlights, there's

a camera and tripod in front of me, my left arm is hanging by my side with the right crooked, holding a cable release attached to the shutter button – not crouched with an AK47...... "What for?" was the next snapped enquiry. "Erm, it's my hobby" I croaked. Pity I couldn't say I was an international spy engaged in undercover espionage of utmost importance, but somehow 'I like taking pictures of lorries' sounds rather lame. "Where are you from?" This time I was able to point like a simpleton and the officer swung on his heels to follow my forefinger.

"I live in Bywater House in the flats over there." Sure enough, half a mile away on the distant hill were the 5 tower blocks of home with warm lights twinkling invitingly. "Why are you out so early in the morning" he snapped, and I sensed he was after his 'I've got you there, villain' moment. "It's so I don't get disturbed by anyone" I retorted, at the same time thinking '…… by people like you' and by that I meant *anyone*, not the Police in particular, who I always respect by default. With that, the questioning was toned down. He went over his enquiries in a different way trying to make sense of my activity. Eventually he realised I was a harmless geezer with a camera, engaged in an odd pastime, so he motioned the other officers to stand down. "It's just someone taking pictures of trucks" he said, a tinge of discernible ridicule in his voice (the police don't enjoy being embarrassed by a fruitless shout, as I've found in the past while being picked up when innocent) and a disappointed "uh, okay" came from the background over a backdrop of garbled messages into radio handsets and the thrum of car engines.

 Crisis averted, I then asked the main officer why they'd been alerted. Apparently a security guard saw me leaving the vicinity of the secure lorry park in my dark clothes and balaclava. Tucked under my arm, the legs of the tripod stuck out like a Sten gun or automatic firearm. He'd alerted the police with the phrase "there's a guy out there acting suspiciously and I think he's got a gun!" which alerted the coppers pronto. I wish I'd taken the time to look around more and soak in the atmosphere but the lights were frankly dazzling. The officer concluded with an apology. Finally there was a multitude of doors being slammed and the amplitude of whining transmissions from various squad cars being slung into reverse. Then, as the last of the tail lights trailed off into the distance; I was back in the street,

standing a bit bewildered with the tripod before me, a still slumbering lorry driver in his cab and the robins chirping noisily in the trees over a backdrop of virtual silence. I can't even remember which lorry I was photographing. It was all a bit of a blur. The whole thing lasted less than ten minutes.

Years later, reflecting on the event, I wondered if any of the officers were armed? I'll never know.

Another night I was approaching the Pleck Road lorry park. To my right on the opposite carriage was a Royal Mail Leyland 10 tonner coming back to base in the early hours. Seemingly without reason, it crashed into a low wall near some traffic lights with a loud 'thud'. It was around 3am and there was not a soul about. The driver seemed unhurt and was more dazed than anything else. I suspect he may have fallen asleep at the wheel. I opened the door and asked if he was alright. Despite his slow assurance that he was, he need to be checked over and the truck removed as the front was somewhat bent. This was before the days of widespread mobile phone usage, at a time when most police stations were manned before wondrous government cutbacks. Quickly, I mounted my bike and pedalled furiously to the nearby police station on Green Lane quarter of a mile away, to alert the slumbering fuzz.

As this is written, the police station is being demolished after 50 years of use. It closed in 2016 and ironically was described in the local paper in early 2019 as being "a magnet of crime"! I won't pass further comment.

Partly in shadow, this shot of two Cardiff Transport tractors came out surprisingly well. I'm guessing the exposure would have been about 4 minutes in June 1992. This was a street I found particularly scary to stand around in, so I would rarely venture up to the right angled corner, except to cycle past. In the foreground is a fairly new MAN F90 while in the back was an older MAN F8 tractor. Both were carrying concrete extrusions.

This Scania 113m with its later spec and more rounded high datum cab was part of the Eddie Stobart fleet. The shot was taken sometime in the mid-nineties in a Walsall back street following a rain shower. The lorry was new and the company has an undeniably photogenic livery.

Chapter 5

FAMOUS FLEETS

The sheer variety of vehicles was part of the anticipation of venturing out at night. It was great to render an independent owner/driver on film but conversely, just as reassuring to see a popular fleet truck and I have included a selection of them here. Depending on where you are in the country, one person's familiar fleet may be relatively unknown to another. Another pleasing aspect was that often I'd witness lorries at night that I would not see in the day. Millicans of Cumbria and Ditchfields for example, were regulars in the darkness but I'd never seen them in daylight. It seemed like a parallel universe from which a different array of road haulage existed.

A well-established fleet is the numerically large WH Malcolm of Brookfield and they have run a variety of makes and types over the years to suit their needs. Always with a nice livery, this handsome 1992 ERF E14 320 was parked up in Long Street, Walsall in 1995 with a Volvo FH12 behind and another ERF E Series behind that.

A famous fleet for sure was Bowkers of Blackburn who used to run predominantly dark blue Atkinsons and later Scanias. What was just once a broad white stripe transformed into a white livery in later years. This fairly plain Volvo FL10, reg. number M704 WLV was photographed when it was brand new in the winter. I like the shot as the reflective thin layer of snow makes it look like it was taken in a studio.

The corrosive values of salt made the anti-rot composite Foden cabs ideal. British Salt of Middlewich used a few ERFs but it was mostly Fodens that were used at the time. This 1984 Foden S104 was photographed in the early nineties I think and number 27 was apparently 'Trev's Truck' according to the signwriting under the screen.

Chris Miller of Preston was a well-established company and had some famous trucks for heavy haulage on the books. These included a 6x4 Mack F700 drawbar tractor and a Thorneycroft Mighty Antar. Alas, nothing so exotic was seen at night. However, this 1979 DAF 2800 would have been a good working tool and was seen parked up early one evening as the sun was setting with a 28mm wideangle lens on an Olympus OM1 that I was trying out.

A warm night in the summer of 1995 made for pleasant picture taking conditions in Walsall. I was passing the Key Fuels diesel pumps and the well-known fleet of WA Glendinning of Durham often had vehicles refuelling there. This brand new ERF EC10 looked great in their traditional maroon and cream livery and was uncommon since the EC Series tractors were only just coming on stream at the time.

George Allinson of Darlington are well known for their heavy haulage exploits and often use 'trombone' extendable trailers for lengthy steel sections. This 1990 Volvo FL10 6x2 tractor and Boalloy Tautliner is an unremarkable fleet lorry but shows off Allinson's distinctive crisp livery. The picture was taken in December 1991 and in the background is the sombre black outline of what was a famous Walsall landmark, the BOAK building tower. Some years later, the whole factory literally burned to the ground in a spectacular fireball. I witnessed it, but never had my camera. Duh!

I like the juxtaposition of these two Geoffrey Reyner ERF E6 rigids. Reyners of Manchester had a large fleet and the familiar livery was a common sight. ERF and Seddon Atkinsons were among the major makes used and the shot was taken with Kodachrome 25 film in January 1994 using a 24mm wideangle lens and around a 4 minute exposure.

F.B. Atkins of Derby were well known for their brown Atkinsons at one time but over the years the fleet was re-liveried in yellow. This 1991 Renault G290 38 tonner was not that common but was typical fare for the mid-nineties and they used to run some Iveco tractors too.

Bewick Transport Services from Milnthorpe in Cumbria used to run a tidy red and white fleet that started with Atkinsons and later ran into Scanias over the years, hauling paper products. This low datum 1990 Scania 113m had the cab in the livery of The East Lancashire Paper Mill. The shot was taken in January 1994 using a 24mm Nikkor wideangle lens on Kodachrome 25 ISO film. I would have got right down on wet knees to get this shot which would have resulted on a chilly ride home. You have to suffer for your art sometimes.

Hills of Cardiff were a frequent sight at the Walsall lorry park and it was nice to see three articulated units together. I used a 28mm wideangle lens to get them all in and with some light in the sky it was around one second to record the trio on film in early September 1990. With over 100 trucks in the fleet, Hills was a sizable concern and there was often a Seddon Atkinson to be seen at the time, like the 401 on the right.

Meachers Transport was formed in 1958 and were major users of ERF lorries. This trio of E Series E14 tractors was typical of the Southampton based fleet in the 1990s.

From Distington in Cumbria, Tyson H. Burridge came to my attention years ago when I photographed a tidy Foden Fleetmaster of theirs. Having decided I liked their two tone blue livery, I was always on the lookout for one of their lorries. Fortune smiled on me as this rare 1982 Spanish Dodge 300 came into view up in Trafford Park, Manchester. The date was November 1990 and the driver was just about to jump into the cab as 'Tarnside Stranger' was sat on the weighbridge.

I deliberately positioned the camera so the traffic lights at the rear of the subject would record the complete red, orange, green countdown as I knew the exposure would be long enough. This was taken at the end of the lorry park that used to be by the Walsall Manor Hospital. This handsome 1989 Cummins 14 litre powered Seddon Atkinson Strato was operated by W&J Riding of Longridge, which was definitely a famous fleet. This shot was taken in January 1994 just a year before the Riding name disappeared. The lorry was called 'Sir Galahad.' The strapline 'The best in the long run' was a nice touch, as a company motto under the windscreen. The exposure was one and a half minutes at F4 with a 50mm lens on Kodachrome 25 film.

The distinctive red, white and black livery of John Raymond Transport of Bridgend with the stylised 'R' wraparound band was a common sight at night. This handsome 1985 Seddon Atkinson 401 was a typical example from the large fleet. It was the early nineties when this sheeted strip steel loaded rig was photographed.

I think this picture was taken around 1990. The large fleet of P&O included the Pandoro division as part of their Irish Sea roll on/roll off services. This ERF C Series 6x2 tractor took around 5 minutes to record on film as indicated by the star trail streaks above the Boally Tautliner trailer. Knowing I would have to stand around for a while, I would probably have picked a summer month to use the Lubitel camera.

Robsons of Carlisle were not long for this world as a going concern by the time this shot was taken, though I didn't see them too often, even in the daytime. Each lorry had the name 'Border' within its name below the screen. 'Border Solway' in this case, was a 1986 DAF 2800 ATI and it was 2.30am in November 1990 when the shot was taken. I had come back to Walsall on a late train from Oxford and walked home after the trip to the lorry park. I wish I had the energy to do such things now, but I'd rather not walk home so late nowadays. Dim lighting meant an exposure of six minutes at 5.6.

'At your service Sir!' was a nice traditional touch, signwritten on the bumper on one of at least 15 ERF EC tractors operated by Jack Richards of Fakenham. Even though original owner Jack has sadly passed, the distinctive yellow livery can still be seen today. This EC11 6x2 tractor was taken with a Mamiya 645 medium format camera, using a 70mm lens and an aperture of F11 with about a three minute exposure in June 1999, making the tractor quite new.

From Skelmersdale in Lancs, Ken Abram Ltd had been in operation since 1962 and used a striking livery across a nice mixed fleet. Both Scania and Mercedes were on the books but this shot highlights a 1995 Renault Magnum and a 1988 DAF 3300 with an angular roof extension. By 1996 Abrams were finished, not long after this photo was taken. It was a winter shot with light snow in the background and brown slush on the lorry park surface. This meant a big weekend clean for the lorries back at base.

I think we can all agree that the vehicles of Eddie Stobart are famous. Whatever one may think of this often controversial haulier, I am happy to include Stobart trucks in the book as they have an undeniably photogenic livery and look good both night and day. It's as simple as that. It would be silly to exclude a Stobart shot for the sake of anyone's prejudice or principle. I photograph Stobart Scanias all the time and they look great. I am dictated to by my own brain. An unlettered fleet truck makes my right arm inert, but if I see colour and lettering, my reflexes kick in automatically as my camera is snapped up to my eyeline. Like Pavlov's dog, I'm conditioned to it. So here's a selection of familiar lorries under the stars. Some readers may even have driven one.

I make no apologies for including more than one Eddie Stobart picture. They are one of the most famous fleets in the world, lots of haulage enthusiasts like Stobart pictures and frankly, I would like the book to sell! This imposing Seddon Atkinson Strato was not that numerous among Stobart lorries and this 1993 example with Boalloy trailer was taken around 1995, lurking in Walsall.

Chapter 6

FROZEN FODENS

Most times, the weather was accommodating if you chose the night wisely. Ideally a cool, clear, still night was ideal. The summer months were good because the sky never gets inky black and the deep blue complemented the amber street lights. Add a colourful lorry and the scene was set for a great photograph.

Wet nights, unless the rain has definitely finished, were to be avoided and windy nights were a no-no for obvious camera shaking reasons. Sometimes I got it wrong and had to cope with conditions as they transpired. One clear night for example, I set off, thinking

I guess this the sort of picture that sorts out the committed photographer from the happy snapper. Maybe I should have been committed for venturing out on such a cold night, but the conditions of Thursday 7th February 1991 were too good to ignore. The daytime had seen freezing winds and dry powdery snow. When I looked at nearby trees and walls, the snow had been hurled horizontally across them, as if from a celestial spraygun. By midnight however, the wind had stopped and I got ready to venture out with the tripod as conditions were perfect for some pictures with drama. I was hoping to see no-one as I wanted virgin snow without footprints. I got my wish as the last flurry covered up any remaining scars on the white surface. I used Kodachrome 25 daylight film as I knew the exposures would be faster in the brighter conditions. Let's hope the night heaters were working on the frozen circa 1989 Hills of Cardiff Leyland DAF 95 and the 1990 MAN F90 of C&G Neve.

Early December 1990 had seen some severe cold weather countrywide and the Midlands received around 7 inches of snow on one particular day. It was a blizzard with a horizontal white wind. I actually went out in it to record this rare phenomenon and got some great black and white urban landscapes in tricky conditions. By nightfall, colour was restored and the breeze dropped. I managed to get this 1985 Seddon Atkinson 401 of Leggett Freightways on Ablewell Street, central Walsall.

Venturing out in the rain was never a good idea, not only for an uncomfortably wet body, but constantly wiping the lens of the camera and condensation was irksome. However, once the showers had stopped, a wet road and water droplets on the bodywork often made for nice images. This 1986 Mercedes SK of well-established Murray Hogg was part of their big fleet from Newcastle-upon-Tyne and they still run Mercedes vehicles today. This shot was taken in a Walsall back street around 1995.

Sometime in the mid-nineties, I was out during one of the winter months as a covering of light snow had recently abated. It was starting to thaw and become rain, so I had to move quickly. This Volvo FH12 was a fairly recent fresh face on our roads and a rigid curtainside variant with a trailer was a rare sight. Bergen Transport of Trafford Park in Manchester operated this imposing Volvo.

the breeze was gentle. Later the wind increased severely. Taking shots on a wild night in the open was impossible. Shame, because the clouds were scudding across the sky, backlit by moonlight, in spectacular fashion. However, I noticed that when I was standing close to the cab in the 'top' lorry park on Pleck Road, the air was relatively still. Behind the lorries was a low bank and beyond that, four storey flats provided a wind break. Employing a wide angle lens, I could get near to the cab using it as shelter. I could only take a few pictures, but the ones that worked were worthwhile.

Soft shoe shuffle

By default, I'd pad around very carefully on the crunchy gravel to get a shot. Sometimes you would automatically suddenly stop still like a cartoon villain, when a driver stirred in his cab. My worry was that he'd suddenly open the door and bellow "Oi, what do you think you're doing!" It never happened of course. Drivers were understandably pooped after a long day at the wheel. Occasionally interiors would be illuminated under the curtains and the contours of a small telly could be seen, but at 3am most, if not all cabs were dark. To get low down to the tripod I often ended up with one wet knee from the damp road which further chilled me. I'd tell myself not to do it, but a

This shot was taken sometime in the early nineties on one of the local lorry parks. Treading around the thin wet snow often led into slush, mud and gravel. It was not particularly pleasant, but that photo of an ERF C Series at night was not going to take itself. Allmans Transport of Congleton used to run ERF B Series and E Series ERFs thereafter, all in a classic dark blue/red chassis livery. This hard grafting 1983 6x2 tractor was hauling fabricated steel sections and the fact that it was Gardner 300 powered, rounded things off nicely.

This shot was taken in the early to mid-nineties and depicts an ERF C Series having shaken off a covering of snow on its journey to Walsall to park up. Hunt Brothers of Culcheth in Warrington had a fleet concentrated on ERFs including M Series rigids and B Series tractors. They ran ERFs right to the end of the marque which demonstrated loyalty. I had my camera tottering on an unsecure snowy footing, with a wideangle lens to get the ERF in the frame.

few shots into a session, I got fed up with craning my neck and contorting my midriff to peer inside the tiny viewfinder, nearly upside down. Eventually I'd drop on both knees to compose the lorry comfortably and get it square in the frame - not at a jaunty angle. Hours later, I'd regret it as damp jeans made for a freezing ride home in the winter months. I was getting close to hypothermia sometimes and shaking uncontrollably by the time I got back, gasping up the hill with dry mouth, powerless legs and frazzled eyes. The pleasure to open the front door of the flat and feel the warm waft of the night storage heater was tangible. I'd leave the camera in the bag to thaw out. If set free from the haversack, condensation would cover the chilled camera body and fog the lens. Fortunately it had no electronics to damage.

Taking photos in foggy conditions was challenging. The diffuse light was atmospheric but diminished visibility meant getting close to the cab. Again, a wideangle lens was ideal, but you had to be extra quiet setting up, carefully removing debris in front of the tyres which might spoil the shot. The Sherlock Holmes backstreet look was great but you couldn't see who was coming out of the shadows. Visibility tapered off into seemingly grey smoke only a few feet away from the lorry. All of this might sound rather daft if reading from the comfort of home. But the sense of fear and foreboding on a cold autumn night with the smell of a warm engine and rubber only three feet away

Although this was a clear night into early morning, the wind had got up and clouds were racing across the sky. I got down low with a wideangle lens and thankfully the John Dee DAF and curtainsider had acted as a giant windbreak to stop the cab of F508 XAV rocking. The unit was an ERF E10 belonging to Pearce Transport of Arrington in Cambs. The bright moon has illuminated the streaked clouds and swaying trees.

I was fortunate to have a brief tour at the yard of Bassetts in Tittensor. RG Basset & Sons are famous Stoke hauliers and were noted for giving their Atkinson Borderers a long life on the road. Nowadays such characterful lorries are long gone, but in February 1990, among the fleet were this collection of Gardner powered ERF C Series tippers with a B Series to the right. The late afternoon sun had illuminated the cab fronts, but ominous dark skies had rendered the background a deep blue/grey. As the heavens were opening up, it was time to scarper!

Derek Horton's 1980 Cummins powered ERF B Series tipper returns back to its Walsall base. The lorry was called 'Intrepid' and the shot was taken at 1/125th of a second at 2.8 on freezing day in December 1991.

It was around 1995 when this quite new Scania 143m 450 was parked up. The lorry park in front of Walsall's cop shop became brighter as fresh fallen snow shone further light at the tractor and trailer. The Thermo King refrigeration unit didn't have to work overtime on the Huntapac liveried trailer in these conditions. W&J Hunter of Tarleton near Preston would have been rightly proud of this rig. I caught it again one clear dry night and it was rather immaculate.

HUNTAPAC

THE SEAL OF QUALITY FRESH PRODUCE

W. & J. HUNTER

TRANSPORT

TARLETON

SCANIA

143M 450

January 1996 was naturally cold but not overly so and turned out to be unusually foggy. Taking shots from any distance would render the lorries increasingly indistinct, the further away I was. I came prepared with a 28mm wideangle lens to get the camera close as possible to the subject. Now the lorry would be sharp and the background soft and hazy which was the effect I desired. However, this meant being extra quiet in both padding around the lorry and setting up the tripod, together with laying down my bicycle. Adding to the likelihood of soiling myself, the thought of anyone suddenly appearing out of the shadows was intensified. I enjoyed the way the lorries looked in the viewfinder during the 'pea-souper', but actually as I inhaled the aroma of cauterised rubber, oxidised steel, stale grease and diesel, I couldn't wait to get out of there! A 1989 Sedd-Atki Strato belonging to Alpine of Ellesmere Port and a Scania 113 of Les Watson Transport of Calthwaite in Cumbria were the unwitting subjects.

felt very real at the time. Especially when you would hear the driver stir in his bunk with a creak. *What am I doing here?* That mantra again.

There were plenty of things that would make you jump. It took a while to get used to night heaters for example. In winter, if a lorry was parked up with traffic around, the noise of a heater starting up would not be of any consideration. However, at 2 am when even drips of water from a tree leaf can be heard, a night heater kicking off sounded like a snorting dragon. The first time I heard one, I recoiled, wondering what the hell was going on. The gurgling hum and steam erupting from under the cab in the cold air was startling. When I got used to it, it was handy for masking the sound of crunching gravel underfoot while moving around the lorry.

In snow, the tripod would sometimes slip as you could not feel what was gravel, grass or Tarmac below the tripod legs. A layer of fresh snow was actually quite grippy as you crunched around the cab and any surrounding activity was muffled. By contrast, wet roads and paving amplified noise so that a dropped plastic lens cap rattled like a bin lid!

It was literally a filthy night when this Sam Longson Ltd ERF E Series bulk tanker was captured for posterity. Normally this would have been a tidy rig, but days of winter road dirt had sprayed the tank body up to midway and I had to tread carefully over the thin ice covering the grubby concrete of the secure lorry park. The shot was taken around 1995 and the tank was loaded with sodium carbonate. Longsons were a well-respected Chapel-en-le-Frith haulage concern and used to run Foden S21 eight leggers many decades ago.

A frozen Foden for sure. This Redland Bricks Foden 4300 is seemingly petrified following the blizzard of February 1991. Kodachrome 25 daylight film tried its best to cope with orangey lighting on a pale green lorry and the results are rather other worldly. Which was partly what I was after. In the morning, my semi-circle of footprints around the lorry may well have looked suspicious as I traversed around my subject in the early hours.

The frozen ice on the ground was in limbo as a gradual thaw made it look like the top of a lemon drizzle cake. This 1989 Scania 93m 280 was a good example of a clean fleet truck and it glowed nicely within the confines of the lorry park. Tetrad of Lancashire make furniture and this high volume trailer would have fitted the bill for the relatively light load. I used a Pentax MX and 28mm 'M' Series moderate wideangle for the shot. This camera and its lens range were noteworthy for their small size and quality, making them ideal for my purpose. The shot was taken on Kodachrome 64 in December 1995.

If you ever wondered why cabs rust, I think this picture illustrates the phenomenon. You can almost see and hear the creeping oxidisation as the rivulets of condensation gently dissolve the cab while the driver sleeps, insulated from steel, chilled from the night air. I've always loved the look of the short wheelbase Leyland/Scammell Roadtrain 6x2 tractors with the diesel tanks tightly wedged in between the wheels. TW Brown of Burnley were the operators of C482 SNR and the photograph of this handsome beast was taken in June 1989.

Two hard working lorries of different vintages brave the elements in this picture. The 1979 ERF B Series with its slightly drooped front bumper huddles in the background while the newer Volvo FL10 of Trans-Moore Haulage seemingly stands with more confidence, basking in the gleam of passing headlights of a frozen night in February 1991 at the lorry park.

Sometime in the mid to late nineties I was up in Preston taking pictures of a dragster belonging to a character called Smax Smith. Knowing I was a truck pervert, he responded to my enthusiasm for the nicely hued fleet of K&P Iddon of Leyland by offering to take me to the yard. Alas, the premises were unsurprisingly shut at night and it was raining. Undaunted I set my camera on the ground under the gates and hoped for the best. I'd have liked it to be pictorially better, but a string of turquoise ERFs among others was better than a poke in the eye with a sharp stick.

The scene looks benign enough but conditions underfoot were a bit dodgy. I was using my moon-on-the-top-of-the-picture technique and with this trio of Volvos, the blue hue matches well. The shot was taken around 1995 with James Soens of Warrington the subject. The FH12 Volvo towering above the FL10s flanking it. While fresh snow is often a delight to walk on and often quite grippy, after a couple of days it turns to slush, then re-freezes and in a lorry park gets churned up by the tyres to become a hard, slippery, lunar landscape. It's not only treacherous to walk over, but in places the ice crunches noisily in the dead of night to ruin the clandestine effect.

Any residual water off the tyres and bumper has frozen and turned to icicles on this Wilds Motors 1984 Seddon Atkinson 401. I can remember taking shot of a Wilds Seddon Atkinson 400 around the same area years before, but that was a summer evening with sunlit reflections. Such a contrast to the conditions of February 1991 as here, with airbrushed snow hurled over the trailer sheeting.

Literally just up the road from the Walsall lorry parks is the small but tidy fleet of Derek Horton. Based in a compact yard in Rollingmill Street, Derek has always been an ERF man and Gardner ERF B Series 8-leggers were some of his earliest tackle, to be replaced by Cummins engines in C, E and EC Series rigids and artics. The loads are predominantly scrap which takes its toll on the equipment but the fleet is always signwritten and well maintained. This picture was taken in December 2014 as part of my university course, since I was covering the subject of time exposures. This fine pair of circa 2004 Foden Alphas with high roof cabs were ready for another days work and were replaced by Renaults as both ERF and Foden are sadly no more.

Chapter 7

MATCHING PAIRS

Along with the pleasure of seeing a familiar fleet truck or a really nice livery, it was always good to witness pairs of vehicles together. Often trucks would be in convoys of two or more on a similar job and would converge later to park up sociably. It made sense especially if a driver knew of a safe place to park up, plus you could chat to your mates, share a cuppa and maybe head off for a welcome beer after a long day. I remember a couple of drivers on summer evenings suggesting I should join them for a pint at the nearby Orange Tree pub frequented by truckers, but respectfully I declined. I regret it in a way, but I was on my bike and I would have had far too much boozy fun! On occasion I would take some pictures in the day and then return at night and it was amazing how the scene had changed. Light skies were now dark and open cab windows letting in warm afternoon air were now shuttered with curtains. Human activity had vanished and ambient sounds changed with only the occasional passing taxi and the ever present robins twittering loudly in the early hours, thinking the street lamps were daylight. Ahead were the same trucks which had previously had doors open and drivers laughing. Now they were dark and silent with the lights from passing vehicles sweeping the cab paintwork, dancing over the shiny contours.

This pair of DAF cabs demonstrate older and newer versions of the same structure. On the extreme left is a 1986 Renault G Series tractor while the DAF units are a 1986 3300 ATI with a 1981 DAF 2800 on the right. The bright orange fleet was that of Roy S. Ely of central Birmingham in the Nechells district of the city. Ely finished in 2010 when the local LDV vans concern failed from where much of the work came. This shot was taken around December 1987 when tipper activity was undertaken. It required an exposure of around a minute under the yard lights.

Sidney C. Banks of Sandy in Bedfordshire were frequent visitors to Walsall and were often in pairs or as here, a convoy of at least three tri-axle tippers. The 1993 Leyland DAF 95 at the head of the bunch superceded the Leyland Roadtrains, two of which are parked behind. The lorries would visit nearby Smiths flour mill and would park up there, on the lorry parks or, as here, in Margaret Street - which was dimly lit and somewhat foreboding at night. The shot was taken in January 1994. As I wanted to get the hell out of there I opened up the lens to F4 to allow more light in. Even then, because the film was 25 ISO Kodachrome, the exposure still took five minutes. At F5.6 it would have been two minutes more and on a lonely, cold January night, I'd had enough standing around.

Head to head, this pair of Volvo FL10 tractors were quite new when then were photographed in January 1994. A fine spray of road filth from the day's travelling activities has weathered the trucks slightly as they slumbered in a Walsall back street.

It was most likely in the early nineties when this pair of 1989 ERF E10 325 tractors were photographed in the lorry park. The units were both named after woodland birds it appears with 'Lakeland Harrier' on the left and 'Lakeland Woodcock' on the right. Cannons of Cumbria were the operators and the nice red and blue livery appeared on Scanias in the fleet as well.

Evans Transport of north Devon has various depots and a large fleet of green and red painted units. They have been keen on Volvos for years and this shot taken in the secure lorry park in Walsall, shows a selection from around 1995. The new FL10 in the centre was flanked by an older 1985 F10 on the right and a newer 1989 F10 on the left. The fact that the loads were logs meant that the trucks were enroute from somewhere not in the locality, which was heavily industrialised rather than forested.

On this occasion I left Dr Watson behind and donned my cape and deerstalker to become Sherlock Holmes for the night. I deduced that taking a shot of two MAN tractors in the fog was a two pipe problem and decided to use a 28mm 'M' Series lens to get the job done. The 1985 6-16-321 tractor in the foreground was accompanied by C842 ONH behind. H. Brown of Barnsley were more noted for their tipper work in my observation, but on this night in January 1996 a Case tractor was the load.

I was pleased with this shot since my double exposure moon technique was often something of a lottery because I was never quite sure where the moon would come out in the top of the frame. In this case, the blue hue matched the tractors and it was fairly central. It was fitting that the livery of Great Bear had its logo reflecting the image of the celestial Great Bear star constellation on this starlit image. The shot depicting a pair of new Mercedes SK EPS V6 tractors was taken between the hours of 1.30 and 3am in February 1995. The moon was taken with a 400mm lens and the lorries ultimately shot with a 50mm lens on a Pentax MX.

I didn't have to travel far to get this pair of ancient Vickers AWD mobile cranes as I would often pass them on my way to the lorry park district. The yard of Walsall Crane Hire Ltd is now long gone, but in December 1993 at well past 1am, I decided to ignore my frozen extremities and give up three and a half minutes of my time dithering to take a picture on Kodachrome 25. This was about the last shot of the night and bed time could not come fast enough.

The P&O Roadways combine out of Felixstowe and other depots has undergone numerous vehicle derivations and livery changes over the years. This pair of P&O Roadtanks DAFs illustrates the old and the new. On the left is a 1988 DAF 2800 with its ubiquitous angular cab which was starting to be phased out. On the right, was a 1990 Leyland DAF 95, the cab architecture of which is still around today. January 1992 was the date and the exposure in a dimly lit corner of the Green Lane lorry park would have been about four minutes on Fuji 64 ISO tungsten balanced film.

What was better than a British truck with a tidy roped and sheeted load at night? A pair of them of course! Actually one night, I really got lucky in much the same place as Peter Halley Transport of Crieff in Tayside had four sheeted wagons parked up including an ERF E Series. I've chosen this shot as it's more concise and it shows off a pair of 1989 Seddon Atkinson 4-11 38 tonners. There was a slight gradient to this part of the lorry park and the exposure was at least three minutes on a Thursday night into Friday morning in March 1995. Halley's appeared to run British tackle right up until when they finished which was commendable. The standout livery also appeared on Seddon Atkinson Strato and ERF EC tractors.

Two different vehicles out at night from the same firm, demonstrating the large and small of cab design. Though both were sometimes classed as fleet trucks, the older Volvo cab is somewhat dwarfed by the later generation ERF E Series. Walpole & Wright of Dereham in Norfolk were the operator though they probably had other depots. The date was June 1992 and just a 10 second exposure was required on 64 ISO tungsten film since new overhead lorry park lights were quite bright. These were located by the machine where the drivers paid for the night. They were actually set on a lower beam, to reduce energy consumption and would only come to full illumination, when someone passed in front of the sensor. In this case, some dork with a tripod.

It was an early evening in June 1993 when these Mercedes SK 2345 Powerliner tractors were photographed. Time for drivers to catchup after a long day at the wheel. T. Brady of Barrow-in Furness were regular visitors, using Walsall as a stopping point and the trailer is sensibly backed up close to the wall to prevent any dodgepots nicking stuff. An Olympus OM1, 28MM Zuiko lens and Kodachrome 64 film took care of the exposure.

Sometimes as many as four Cardiff Transport tractors hauling steel would be parked up at night in Walsall. This pair of well-worked 1988 MAN tractors were parked up sometime in the morning back in the early 1990s, having possibly been up to Scotland.

The appropriately named S&K Haulage of Barry in South Wales ran these Mercedes V6 SK tractors, though they have commonly run Volvos. This pair of tankers was photographed around 1996 and the exposure was sufficiently long to render all three colours of the traffic lights visible.

This trio of Scania 142m tractors was an image that got damaged but I wanted to include it because it summed up the atmosphere of lorries refuelling at the Walsall Keyfuels station at night. The operator was Connolly Transport of Ballymoney, Northern Island and it was May 1990 in the early hours when the picture was taken.

An unusual but sensible place to park up was near the Jewson builders merchants in Rollingmill Street, Walsall. My cheapo Russian Lubitel was pressed into service to record a pair of trucks belonging to Baxi, the makers of boilers. Both were immaculate. A new 1993 Cummins powered Seddon Atkinson Strato on the left partnered with a 1989 Seddon Atkinson 4-11. The different generations of cab design can clearly be seen. The big orange flare on the top left is from the street lamp, rather than an alien invasion.

This is one of my favourite images and a shot with which I was confident of the outcome - for a change. I took multiple pictures, bracketing the exposure to ensure success. It was a clear night and in one of the best illuminated sections of the lorry park, I spied a Holy Grail opportunity, namely a pair of photogenic Brian Harris ERFs. I used a 28mm wideangle on a Pentax MX to get both lorries in and hunkered down low, both to prevent flare from the street lamp behind and to encourage a halo effect around the subject. Two Cummins powered 1989 ERF E Series tractors, 'Phantom of the moor' and 'Peter Davey' were beautifully signwritten and pinstriped in traditional fashion. The exposures were between 6 and 18 seconds and the photograph was taken around 3am on Thursday 21st September 1995.

Chapter 8

UNDER THE SHEETS

Part of the fascination of lorries is the traditional image of a sheeted load. There are many ways goods can be carried but there's something very characterful about a roped and sheeted shroud. The mystery of what's under the tarp seems to be magnified at night. A dark and sinister hump on the trailer was often in matt black, green or blue, in contrast to the shiny cab. 'What's he got under there?' I'd wonder. Sometimes it was fairly obvious, like the rounded profile of large paper rolls which invariably were stacked pretty high. Other times there was the random shape of some oddball machinery. Most often, it was simply an elongated envelope, sometimes with the hauliers' logo and the load could be anything from boxes of machined parts to bottled drinks. Either way, the neatness of some wrapped loads had to be marvelled at. Since I was the only person out there during a long exposure, I would have plenty of time to stare and admire the drivers' handiwork. The least I could do was take a picture to record this

I know that H&G Haulage of Wigan used to haul paper as well as steel extrusions and this 1988 Seddon Atkinson 4-11 tractor appears to be piled high with papyrus rolls under the tarp. A still night in November 1995 around 2am made for good photographic conditions.

A rare sight even in December 1991, it was a tricky shot to take because the subject was both backlit and had light spillage. Flare from the illuminated diesel pump and the lorry headlamps had to be considered. This 1977 Scania 86 was the Swedish manufacturer's initial foray into the rigid six-wheeled market and RHS 704 seems to have been originally operated by Mellor of Leek which is faintly legible under the translucent headboard. The driver waiting for the tank to fill, has been rendered almost as a ghost image during the long exposure at the Keyfuels pump.

I liked the subject so was hoping for a good picture. Thankfully it came out as envisaged. Geo. Beer and Sons of Swansea used to run some nice ERFs and Seddon Atkinsons. A clear night and a relatively empty lorry park in September 1995 enabled me to get the whole rig in the shot. The lorry was an ERF E14, reg. number D52 HHM and around two minutes would have secured the exposure.

Around 1998 these two Scanias were recorded on Long Street in Walsall. The lead truck was a high datum Scania 113 belonging to Eric Nicholson of Cockermouth in Cumbria. I deliberately set the camera on the pavement to get a low angle and luckily it was dry so I didn't get my knees wet. The load appears to be bagged compost under the sheeting.

This formidable 1985 Mercedes SK 2033 was run by established haulier T. Brady and Son of Barrow –in-Furness and appeared to be stacked with large paper rolls. This was a common sight overnight for the demands of newsprint. The lorry was parked up in December 1991 in a Walsall back street.

transient artistry. Sometimes on a wet night I'd think of the hapless driver getting to his destination later that day. He'd have to untie sodden ropes, wet straps and sheets that would probably erupt in water from a hidden puddle when let loose. One particularly frosty night led me to consider that the ropes would be frozen by morning and due to the chill factor of the lorry at speed would remain that way, even at its destination with the daytime temperature rising.

Although the lorry park was the obvious place to be for an abundance of trucks, the back streets are where the occasional gem lurked. And fair play to the driver who could find a nice quiet spot to spend the night without disturbance and save a couple of quid in parking fees.

Quality Street

I had a fairly basic flashgun called a Starblitz. It wasn't powerful or sophisticated and would often underexpose pictures. It looked like a professional gun with a tilting head but I felt it was of little worth. I'd use it at full power to occasionally fill shadows under trailers and chassis to reveal detail. An example would be strong street lighting coming from the left. When viewed from the front, anything to the right of the lorry was in deep shadow. Flash balanced out the exposure and added light, to reveal a more complete vehicle.

I would rarely use conventional flash as main lighting though. The technique for using flash off-camera is often called 'painting with light'. During exposures lasting a minute or more, there was ample time to fire off a couple of flashes. To take the George Beer Foden shot in chapter 4 for example, I'd decide how long I wanted the exposure to be and wind on the film. Then wait until the second hand came up to the full minute on my watch.....and hit it! Because it was so quiet, the click of the camera shutter

Preston Van Transport used to run this Leyland Roadtrain of around 1987 vintage. The shot was taken sometime in the mid-nineties and as the newer lighting was brighter, the film only took about 20 seconds to expose.

This 1989 Volvo FL10 was parked up near the railway line. On this occasion it appeared to have the car park to itself, though often it was busy with trucks side by side, like sardines in a tin. Jas. K. Callaghan was the operator from Falkirk who used to run a Volvo F12 Globetrotter as well. The date was June 1992.

This particular night in January 1992 was breezy, sending cloud cover scurrying across the moon. On the left a C. Butt of Northampton Volvo F6 16-tonner was parked, while a hefty ERF C Series twin steer is loaded high with what may be rolls of paper. Draper's Transport of Grays in Essex was the operator, who used to run numerous AECs and latterly Ivecos, among other makes. An exposure of 1 minute, 20 seconds at F4 was relatively quick, so as to negate the risk of camera shake in the breeze.

opening was clearly audible. The cable release (I wore out three of them!) sometimes came with a lock which I'd apply, keeping the shutter open. I'd then walk into position with the flash gun charged and stand about ten feet away. In the case of the Geo. Beer Foden, I fired two flashes at full power, waiting around 15 seconds for the flash to re-charge each time. The first was aimed at the head of the trailer, then I'd crab sideways and fire off another halfway down. For this particular shot I had one minute in which to scuttle back. After checking the watch to see if a minute had elapsed, I'd unlock the cable release to close the camera shutter. If I kept moving when in front of the camera, my image would hardly be recorded on film. Just like a ghost.

Consolidated of Port Talbot used to run some steel haulage tackle and this twin-steer 1989 Mercedes 2028 SK tractor looked purposeful as it parked outside the Long street timber yard one night. A heavy, single coiled strip steel lump sat in the middle of the well trailer.

In April 1991 I bought a secondhand Olympus OM1 camera and took it out for its first roll of film to see if it functioned. A 1979 ERF B Series belonging to Wood and Butler Transport of Blackburn made an impressive subject in the fading light. Especially with a piled high load, sheeted and roped to make an imposing shroud on the trailer.

Ian Craig Haulage are based in Bonnybridge Scotland and specialise in brick/block and timber transport. Nowadays they have a number of Scanias on the books but in January 1994 this 1989 Leyland DAF 95 was in the fleet. The 'Broomhill Flyer' had its load properly protected on this particular damp night in Walsall.

The lorries of Jos. Millican of Longtown in Cumbria were frequent visitors to Walsall at night. I got down low to prevent camera shake with a wideangle lens and the exposure was about half a second in the fading twilight. This was June 1993. Millicans used to run ERFs too but this Cummins powered 1987 Leyland Roadtrain 6x2 was a particular favourite.

A-One transport of Leeds ran a big fleet at one time but the red of the cab is somewhat muted under the overtly orange street lighting. There is some blue in the sky despite the early hours, caused by the background floodlamps of a nearby 24 hour auto recovery service. The Volvo FL10 with its load stacked high, is a 1988 model and the shot was taken in December 1991.

It took around 20 minutes of work to get this spectacular 1989 Scania 113m successfully on film. Set in the dark backwaters, I took a few pictures to ensure success and while two minutes was too dark an exposure, only this shot of some five minutes duration came anywhere close to doing the lorry justice. Stewart Machinery Removals of Manchester were the operators and it was November 1993 when the picture was shot.

Sometimes a lorry frontage was in deep shadow. In this instance, I would never fire the flash directly at the cab but always from the side at an oblique angle for two reasons. Firstly, the lighting would be flat and not naturalistic if fired head on. Secondly, flash would reflect off the number plate making it often unreadable and looked naff. At something like an 80 degree angle, flash was relatively inconspicuous. However, there was a problem. I was photographing in yellowy orange light, and using tungsten balanced film to take most of the colour cast out. The gun had its electronic flash tube balanced for daylight. Light would therefore come out rather blue and look odd. You could obtain both orange and yellow filters to go over the flash head to compensate, but I felt these would be too opaque and would reduce the power of my already puny flashgun.

So, sat home one Christmas, I came up with a solution, having stuffed my face full of Cadbury's

Phil Jenkins was a local haulier to me, being based in Bilston near Wolverhampton. I'd spied this 1984 ERF C Series 6x2 steel hauler a couple of times, at the bottom of the Walsall tower block where I lived. This was sometime in the mid-nineties and I like the lone Ford Fiesta with its rear light twinkling in the background.

A 1987 Scania 112m 38 tonner with its low datum cab was a pleasing shot to take on the tarmac apron in front of some factory units. The lorry with its roped and sheeted load was evenly lit. DA Harrison of Wigton in Cumbria was the haulier concerned and the photo was taken in 1997.

Roses and Quality Street chocolates. Billy Connolly would apparently never trust a man who walked into a room and when faced with a tea cosy, would not put it on his head. I'd think ill of someone who has not put a cellophane sweetie wrapper over their eyes and marvelled at the world rendered red, purple or yellow! Childishness aside, a yellow Quality Street wrapper once applied to the flash head with adhesive tape might work because it was thin, wouldn't absorb much light and wasn't too opaque... so I tried it. And it worked perfectly. The now yellow tinged flash light matched the surrounding street lamps. Consequently, I got fatter and found an original way of getting decent natural looking shots on a budget.

The first time I tried flash to fill in the shadows I was nervous. I didn't want to incur the wrath of a driver, prematurely awoken by some loon, walking around his lorry with an electronic device in his glove, Sellotape flapping disconcertingly over a sweet wrapper. But no-one ever woke up. I figured that so long as I was quiet, since the light looked yellowish, it would only seem like passing car headlights.

Barnes & Tipping of Clitheroe in Lancs were frequent lorry park visitors and three or four lorries of theirs were often around. This 1980 ERF B Series had a red signwritten sheet over the load and my contrived full moon over the factory roof did the picture justice. The shot was taken around two o'clock in the morning in February 1995, meaning that the venerable B Series had endured a long working life.

One particular night, I'd come away from a photo session and for convenience, stuffed the flashgun into my coat pocket (still turned on as it transpired) and pedalled off home. The coat was made of a slippery synthetic material and had no zip. Subsequently, the flashgun tumbled out with a clatter onto the damp main road. Quickly, I pulled on my brakes, moved over to the side and set about retrieving the hapless device. I could see it looking vulnerable near the middle of the road, its red 'on' light winking. Just then, a car came by. I gazed helplessly as the flashgun to my dismay, crunched under the tyres of the car, which continued on its way. In its final seconds, the flashgun let out a dying burst of light to discharge itself. Though irrelevant, I recall it was a Renault 25 that did it in. 'Oh well, the flash was never that good anyway', I reflected, scraping the crushed plastic, mushed battery and wires from the greasy road. I replaced it with a second hand Olympus T32 flash and it worked far better in every way. This enabled me to take reliable flash pictures for car magazine features years later and so paid for itself many times over. Every cloud, etc.

This 1988 ERF E14 Cummins tractor belonged to Walsh and Dearden who are commercial vehicle dismantlers of Darwen in Lancashire. The shot was taken sometime in the mid-nineties I think and it would have been a couple of minutes exposure to get the lorry on film.

At the time I was taking night pictures, roped and sheeted loads were still fairly commonplace and this is a fine example of the truckers skills. Whether or not a load was secured, with adequate knots and the tarp in the right place, fly sheeting done properly etc. is not for me to comment. My camera was there to record in some ways a lost art. The subject was a 1986 Leyland Roadtrain 6x2 tractor in the livery of Hepworth Refractories. Looking closely, the yellow tarp reveals the stencilled lettering of the previous operator that Hepworth took over, GR Stein. They ran a number of these lorries painted yellow.   The dateline was June 1992 and required an exposure of two and a half minutes at F5.6.

Chapter 9

WHEN THE DAWN BREAKS

Just as early evening becomes nightfall, when the sun begins to rise, whether behind cloud or in a clear sky, the reverse happens. This might be stating the obvious, but photographically, there's little difference between pictures taken at dusk or dawn since the light quality is much the same. In fact if I didn't mention the time of day that some of the following shots were taken, one would be hard pressed knowing it was morning or night.

I remember being dropped off in Oxford early one winter morning. I'd stay overnight after a beery drag racing club meeting with a man called Geoff Martin who worked at a local builder's yard. He'd deposit me in the city centre to wait for the first coach back to Birmingham. Rather than just loiter, I'd walk the streets looking for pictures and as dawn broke I got shots of brewery drays in deep blue light before sun-up and a frost encrusted Royal Mail Leyland Chieftain, among others. Sometimes I wish I didn't have the need for sleep and I could go out all the time.

Sometime around the turn of the century (!) I had gone down to West Drayton in Middlesex to photograph a drag racing car. I went on the train and was late getting back, ending up at Worcester. Having miscalculated, there were no trains back until the following morning. Needing sustenance, I decided to feed my face at an Indian restaurant and walk 4 miles through the night to get to Droitwich. At 2am there was not a soul around so I pressed on to Bromsgrove a further 5 miles away. Enroute I spied this 2003 Renault filling up at a pitstop not far from the M5 and asked to take a picture. I'm guessing it would have been around 5am and my bag with camera gear is sat on the left of the picture. Steel haulier A. Hingley of Brierley Hill in the Black Country was the operator and they still run Renaults to this day.

Chas B. Pugh of Wednesbury near Walsall in the Black Country has been established since 1919 and still operate in the scrap metal arena. This characterful Seddon Atkinson 400 skip lorry was seen often. In January 1989 on my way to work, I had my Lubitel 6x6 box camera with me and managed to get a decent shot in the low light.

I used to do factory work in Electric Avenue, Witton - a district of Birmingham, which is where this 1980 Seddon Atkinson 400 came from. The operator was RTZ Metals who I think had various depots and I barely had time around 7.45am to get a photograph before clocking on to earn more peanuts.

Colour was starting to return to the sky as dawn broke over another working day in Oxford back in January 1987. Morrells Brewery had been in existence over 200 years but sadly closed in the nineties. I was waiting for a coach home to Birmingham and propped myself by a lamppost to steady myself during a half a second hand-held exposure of this 1981 Leyland Boxer dray. I deliberately waited for a passing car's headlamps to pass, before pressing the shutter button.

I had little control over the subject as the lorries in my pictures were captured on film just as they sat, without exception. None were moved to get a better picture. Within limitations, I could position myself to eliminate any extraneous elements in the picture. If the background was a bit ugly as was often the case, I would just crop the lorry tighter in the shot. Often I'd spend a couple of minutes adjusting the tripod and camera to get the vehicle square in the viewfinder. Sometimes I would do this laboriously five or six times, checking again and again, to make sure I didn't chop off any part of the subject. Satisfied, I'd check one last time, since it was easy to defocus the lens and ruin the shot. Tricky when it was a dark lorry in the shadows. Address the permutations and be consistent was the key. Often I would have the exposure worked out for the following picture while taking the present one.

Around August 1990 I had taken shots of these two trucks in the daytime and returned at night so as to get this unusual Mack Ultraliner on film. I'm not sure who the operator was, they may have been Dutch, but it contrasted nicely with the AA Lock of Kent MAN tractor.

Night was turning into morning when this 1987 Renault G Series 6x2 tractor was getting ready to hit the road again. Tyson H. Burridge of Distington, Cumbria always had a worthwhile fleet to photograph and this bulk tanker called 'Tarnside Farmer' was one of a couple of Renaults I saw at night. The shot was taken in 1994 and would have taken at least two minutes to render on Fujichrome 64T film.

This Bedford KM tipper had done around a decade's worth of work when photographed early on in 1990. This example has the name 'Tony' signwritten below the screen and is one of those lorries that was largely ignored at the time but was nice to record on film while at work in Birmingham. P. Holloway of Dudley was the operator and I believe they had at least one more KM on the books.

Around 1990, the last of the venerable Scammell Routeman 8x4 tippers could still be seen earning their corn. This one of 1974 vintage belonged to Myles Creek Excavating of Birmingham and was parked next to the ubiquitous JCB, mud plugging on site in the morning. This was doing some work around Witton railway station in Brum and like many Scammells of this era, was probably secondhand.

Shaw's Transport of Lindale in Cumbria ran this sharp looking DAF 3300 ATI. They used to run MAN F90s too. The shot was taken in September 1990 and required around a two second exposure.

I'm not sure of the exact year I took this but I was lurking around the yard of Richard Read in Longhope, Gloucestershire, sometime in the 1990s. Among their extensive range of modern ERF tractors and wreckers was this restored ERF LV delivery van that used to be a mobile shop representing Oldham Batteries. It later served as a parts vehicle. I used to take family holidays nearby the Richard and Harold Read yards, committing various ERFs to film.

Though a January morning can be uninspiring for taking photographs under leaden skies, the artificial lights from various sources can add a little colour to proceedings. For some reason, Leyland stopped putting badges on the front of their T45 range to differentiate between models. Though still modern, they looked a little bland. This Leyland Freighter 17 tonner belonged to Viamaster of Bradford and their nice orange livery cheered up the lorry's looks while parked up in Birmingham.

January 1989 found me working in a factory in the Witton district of Birmingham. I got off the bus around 7.30am and walked around a mile to clock on. En-route, I spied this roped and sheeted ERF B Series belonging to Frank Burton of Gomer Street in Willenhall. The Black Country haulier had an unregistered B Series among other B, C plus E Series tractors and this may have been the one, with its 1985 plate. Either way, I was glad to get a shot of it sat on a damp road, using slow 50 ISO Fujichrome slide film, hand held

I was pleased with this shot and used a graduated filter to add a little colour in the sky to do justice to this brand new, shiny 1996 Seddon Atkinson Strato. Ditchfields of Preston in Lancashire used to run Sedd-Atki 401 tractors and with a machine this smart, it's a shame and a surprise that the Seddon Atkinson company failed.

Working with a tripod slows you down. This can be a good thing as it allows you to literally focus on the composition of the photograph. Each frame started again from scratch to focus the lens, cock the shutter, decide on the exposure, then set the cable release (the integral lock was handy to stop your thumb going numb on a six minute exposure!) It was tiring and laborious when you'd commenced at midnight and it was now three in the morning. I had to keep my concentration levels up to prevent complacency and mistakes. Also, I literally had to look after myself. There was no-one covering my back and when you are on your knees, someone could be potentially behind you in seconds. Thinking about it, put me on edge. Though often lonely, there was a warm feeling of exclusivity in capturing something that no-one else was seeing. This was part of the motivation. Okay, so a mud spattered DAF 2800 and a flatbed trailer may not be everyone's cup of tea, but its' better than yet another shot of the Eiffel Tower when in Paris. You really had to be there at the time and majority of people would rather not I suspect. Suddenly, that paid photoshoot in a warm air conditioned studio photographing models with an assistant looked like a real fantasy. In my case it was. I'd never had such an opportunity. In case anything went shit-shaped, I always kept my bike either propped near where I was working or laid down on the ground next to me. Just in case........

This 1980 Scania 111 tractor shot is made effective by the use of a low angle. I placed the camera on the ground which has rendered the sky a rich deep blue to compliment the orange and tawny hues in the rest of the picture. The owner of the Scania was David Faragher of Stockport. The picture was taken one Monday night around 1990 with a robust but fairly challenging to use Halina 6x6 medium format camera. The aperture used was small to get the most out of an average lens on the camera. Because of this, the exposure was some 6 minutes long. Adequate time to consider what on earth you are doing with your life, standing around the back streets of Walsall at 1.30am.

Chapter 10

INSIDE AND OUT

Although many of my pictures were taken in the lorry park with the express purpose of going out at night, on a lot of occasions I would find myself by a darkened garage or out somewhere at nightfall. Often I had no intentions of taking lorry photos at all, but the sun had dipped and there was the subject.

My clockwork camera would only go down to a timed shutter speed of one second and I had to get creative whenever I didn't have my tripod. Sometimes I'd place the camera on the ground, supporting the lens, angled up, using keys from my pocket, a packet of tissues, a cigarette carton, a couple of flat stones, a twig….. whatever was to hand. Necessity is the mother of invention as they say. I got used to the sensation of sharp gravel imprinting into hands and knees, my ear pressed to the ground, squinting through half an inch of viewfinder glass at a 90 degree angle.

While I was at college in July 2013, I decided to do a photo essay on road menders at night. I'd been tipped off that there was local road resurfacing going on at Walsall town centre and the subject looked ideal. This is one of the few digital photos in the book and it took a 3 second exposure using a basic but capable Nikon D40 6-megapixel camera with an 18-55mm standard zoom. Nothing special, inexpensive, did the job. The shot depicts a Volvo FH12 belonging to National Road Planing and the Wirtgen road planer had just been loaded just before 1am following a road ripping stint.

September 1991 found me in Essex signwriting a Dodge Dart drag racing car. During a break, I spied this ERF E Series tanker so decided to get my camera, plonk it on the ground and hope for a decent shot. The 1990 E14 belonged to United Molasses of London and looked to be parked up for the night.

I was cycling through the Darlaston district near Walsall one Saturday in November 1991. I spied this steel hauling ERF E14 and using a 135mm telephoto lens, attempted to get some shots in the fading light through some railings. Kodachrome 64 and a sharp lens wide open did the trick.

Grubbing around on road surfaces can be a sordid affair. I learned early on to always check the foreground after taking a pit shot of a dragster motorbike in 1980. Supposedly I had the bike lined up in frame looking just dandy. When the prints came back, I hadn't noticed the ugly Coke can right in front of the tyre. Using Photoshop, one can now digitally erase unwanted artefacts from a shot, but during my analogue years of film, the very existence of digital cameras and software programs was inconceivable.

Even the smoothest road surface had grease, tar, oil, grit, stones and diesel to contend with. The terrain in the lorry park or on verges gave you potholes - often water filled, sticks, odd clumps of grass, weeds, bits of rope, broken brick, random newspapers, crisp packets and so on. Once you slipped around the back of a sometimes filthy trailer with limited access, you had to try and get on the next shot, avoiding low walls and stanchion fencing, assorted lumps of concrete, discarded work boots and plimsolls, lengths of bent wire, a wooden leg (not true!) etc. These were regular obstacles that either had to be avoided or dealt with.

When I say dealt with, I mean physically removed. Sometimes it was a simple sweep of the foot to clear autumn leaves and stones. Before you was a shiny new sign-written truck, its tyres with barely a scuff mark on them, parked perfectly, gleaming on an expanse of clean, rain washed road. Satisfied at this paragon of lorry loveliness before you, the tripod was a pleasure to set up in anticipation of the perfect shot. The lens is focussed….. and then you look at the front wheel. A few inches from the sidewall of the Michelin, below the front door was something wretched that needed to be picked up. By hand. Quietly.

This 1971 ERF LV may will have started life as a conventional tractor but by February 1998 when the picture was taken, it served as a showman's drawbar unit. This was Masham in north Yorkshire and it would have formed part of the annual Steam Fair held in the town. My truck driving brother Adam lived there. We'd been to the pub and it would have been rude not to capture 'Barmy Super Bob', as we shuffled home.

Sometime around 1990 I was going on a local night walk around where I lived in Great Barr Birmingham. Parked up near a garage was a Renault 16/17 ton flatbed with a roped and sheeted load. This traditional looking wagon was a development of the Commer Commando and was operated by AG Lowe who had a small depot in Smith St., right in the centre of the city.

When the sun sets or rises, a pretty orange pink glow is often painted on the sky. It can make any subject in the foreground look attractive though it would have to be working hard to make this almost derelict BMC/Leyland Clydesdale tanker look good. An ex-fuel oils machine, I think it belonged to Thomas Clayton (Petroleum Products) Ltd of West Bromwich originally. I was walking by the Leigh Environmental effluent disposal/landfill site in Stubbers Green near Aldridge in Staffs in 1989. The tanker may have been used for water to keep dust down which is a common use in quarries. Certainly well worked, it had seen better days.

Starr Haulage of Vulcan Road in Bilston had an intriguing fleet that was a mix of old and new lorries with Volvos and ERFs always in the mix. On this occasion the Black Country haulier was transporting a new build railway carriage, from the nearby Washwood Heath rolling stock works I reckon. This shot of a 1977 Volvo F88 and a Broshuis extendable trailer was taken around 1988 in fading light on Aston Expressway in central Birmingham.

Around 1997 I was returning from photographing a land speed record attempt up in Elvington Airfield in Yorkshire. We took a break in a layby and alongside us was a 1991 Leyland DAF 95 heavy haulage tractor, also resting. It belonged to GE Curtis of Middlesborough. The load was a Class 20 locomotive aboard a low loader and a dramatic sight it looked too.

This photo was taken in December 1989 when the Harold Read concern was thriving. Specialising in scrap metal, the all ERF fleet always looked presentable with its signwritten maroon livery. They were based in the village of Longhope in Gloucestershire not far from the famous Richard Read concern. This 1984 Cummins powered ERF C Series had just tipped its load in the Black Country town of Wednesbury, its empty trailer body slowly descending as it sped away. I used 1/125th of a second shutter speed and flash to capture the lorry.

I was walking through Birmingham City centre in February 2015 and luckily had my compact digital camera with me. In fading light, I managed to capture this Foden Alpha which was run by A. Pearson and Sons of Coventry. Pearson always found favour with Foden tippers for many years and why not? Foden always made great eight leggers. This one was driven by a character called 'Geordie' according to the yellow number plate barely visible in the cab screen. It also has a subtly signwritten 'why aye man' lower left of the Foden kite emblem.

In November 1990 I was up in Trafford Park, Manchester and was enthralled how much industrial activity there was – including lorries. I was not up there long but managed to get this low datum cabbed Scania 112 as it turned out of a corner using a flashgun. The nice livery employed by Millers of Leyland was highlighted in the gloom.

In February 1996 I paid a repeat visit to the premises of DJ Leddingon in Kingswinford, which is not far from Dudley in the Black Country, Sadly, the owner (and a real gent) John Leddington is not with us anymore. John had an affinity with Seddon Atkinson tractors and performed his own maintenance on a small but immaculate fleet that was always signwritten and pinstriped. Hauling mostly steel, this 1987 example called 'Knight of Honour' was photographed using a fisheye lens to get the tractor within the confines of the garage.

I didn't mind the strip of kebab meat hanging artistically from the Styrofoam food box or the quarter-filled cold tea sloshing around in the disposable cup under a half-on plastic lid. The orange streak of Fanta as it vacated its floppy container, squashed on the Tarmac. A few chips, sailing solo on a sea of swirling ketchup, bobbing on an undercurrent of rain diluted vinegar in the carton. No, it was the discarded kitchen roll and tissues. The image of the stubble-chinned driver delicately dabbing the corners of his mouth after his evening's quality repast, followed by a hearty beer-gas propelled belch was okay. No problem with his wife's long-flung industrial neoprene ham sandwich, curled with grit encrusted butter, making a slippery exit towards a drain. No, it was crumpled tissues. Was it the damp of the road you just felt between your fingers just then – or was it something else? *Something unmentionable!* Eeeeeeuyuk! Without exception, I'd gingerly pick it up and hope it didn't stick to the fingers. Nothing's gonna spoil my picture. No Sir! Luckily, I never contracted anything………

In September 1988 I had the task of delivering some photographs to an office in Fleet Street on behalf of a racing team. It was a Saturday afternoon and I was surprised how quiet it was out of office hours. I decided to walk through some London streets and was rewarded with this rare 1973 Foden S39 eight wheeled concrete mixer. It was all I could do to get a reasonable shot at dusk using slow 50 ISO slide film but it was a treat to see such a handsome machine. Marcon (RMC) was the operator.

Around April 1989 I was in the Black Country town of Oldbury mooching around for pictures, when I noticed this rather smart Scammell Routeman eight wheeled soft drinks dray. Locally they were in Coca Cola livery, but this 1980 example was in the rival Pepsi colours. Having asked permission, I went around this machine diligently to record it for posterity.

One evening in November 1993, I was on a train to nearby Stourbridge to deliver some artwork I'd done. While idly looking out of the window, I spied an Atkinson Borderer. This rare sight got my attention. I got off the train at Lye, (a stop early from my destination) to see if I could locate it. A 1975 example, it was in the livery of DV Williams of Dawley in Shropshire. I spoke to the driver to get some snaps and waited till he got in the cab to fire off my flash to get this shot of him in his rigger boots. The lorry has since been restored.

Light was starting to diminish as I was finishing off a photographic session in Sandbach, Cheshire. Home of the ERF, it was fitting that I was taking shots of mostly B Series like the 1979 model in the picture and a 240 Gardner powered 1973 A Series on the right. F. Hackney was the haulier and I had arranged with owner Howard Hackney to come up to Sandbach in February 1992. Howard and his mother Eliza were most obliging, even making me dinner, which is a reminder of the decent folk who work in haulage.

In February 1988, I went to see my brother in Masham North Yorkshire. I was walking around the town to take in a clear night and passed by the yard of I'Anson Brothers who did animal feeds. Their turquoise with purple trim livery is very attractive and they had some nice Fodens in the yard. However, I was taken with this shot of a Volvo FL6 curtainsider rigid. I used a 180 degree angle fisheye lens to create a little drama and Kodachrome 200 film. The distant moon can just be seen above the roof.

Taking low light shots of a moving vehicle is always a risk. It's okay with digital, but film can be a costly experience with a high failure rate. Who dares wins as they say and with Kodachrome 64, the lens nearly wide open at F2.8 and 1/125th of a second shutter speed, I felt it was worth the risk. Taken in December 1991, this care worn 1985 Mercedes SK 1628 run by Thompson Jewitt International was negotiating a Walsall roundabout on its way back to Nottingham.

In 1986, I'd captured this battered Leyland Marathon tanker in the north of Birmingham on a sunny day. The following year I found that it lived not far from my regular route into the city centre so decided to hunt it down. That November, I found myself in the garage at night and did my best to get WOJ 310T on film. Whelan had an oil reclamation depot and used to run a 1980 ERF B Series tanker as well.

In January 1990 I was traipsing through the outer reaches of Dudley and was feeling tired. However, I perked up when I saw this 1980 Seddon Atkinson 400 parked by the weighbridge of a steel processors. The driver looked like he was fed up with waiting and keen to get back to Yorkshire and the yard of Hillstate Ltd of Rotherham. The element of chance and being on foot oftens pays off.

Coming away with the spoils of war from another night's shuffling around commercial vehicles, I'd treat myself on the ride home with a little game to round off proceedings. Very often the night trunkers were coming though the town on the ring road delivering newsprint and parcels. I could hear an articulated behemoth coming to stop with hiss of airbrakes at the traffic lights behind me. I'd then pedal like the clappers to try and make the last set of lights to beat him and peel off to the quiet street that led home. So off I'd go, pretending the lorry was chasing me down, like a drama, the determined driver set on my destruction, as in the film Duel. But in the dead of night, sound is magnified. The sound of a Scania 142 V8 went from a distant throaty echo into a loud cacophony, then a terrifying roar as it drew level with me. Game over. I'd nearly crap myself, while the oblivious driver got on with checking his mirrors and getting out of Dodge!

Rounding off the book is a selection of pictures in various places where I gladly made the effort to record a worthwhile commercial in random situations.

As I disembarked a train in Stourbridge back in December 1993, there were roadworks underway. I stuck around with my camera to look at some Leyland Reiver tippers from local haulage concern Male & Son of Pensnett, near Brierley Hill. Male used to run Leyland Marathon tractors too. The driver of this Reiver was one John 'Buster' Emmery of Wall Heath. It had stood unregistered for a while, hence the late registration plate. I used a slow shutter speed and flash to get a shot of John at work. (Thanks to Martin Beswick for the info.)

William Stevens in the Black Country ran this AEC Marshall which I believe had been in storage with its original owners but was then put back to work. Now run by William Stevens of Old Hill near Dudley, the green cast of the interior fluorescent lighting can be seen in this shot. The old lorry looked immaculate and hauled steel products by day.

Howard E. Perry of Willenhall ran a pair of handsome green Scammell Crusaders. The picture was taken in their steel mill premises back in February 1988 as Crusaders were getting thin on the ground by that time. I had no problem in obtaining permission and used my tripod and Kodachrome 25 film to get some quality images. Sadly this one was destined for a nearby scrapyard but I also got some snaps of its decay.

In December 1991 I decided to take a pilgrimage up to the yard of Sidney Harrison and pay homage to the high priests of Gardner and Scammell. Like many, I had read about Harrisons and their fleet of awesome Scammell Highwayman tractors in Truck magazine years before. Having spotted them coming to Walsall, I phoned the Harrison brothers and asked permission to come up and take pics. The train journey indicated freezing conditions, but the long day spent with them and Sidney himself yielded some great pictures. This one of a recently refuelled 1968 example was taken as the sun set. It made the centrespread in Heritage Commercials magazine.

In March 2002, I was up in Masham having a beer with my brother Adam at the Kings Head Hotel. When I looked outside, I saw this fairly new Mercedes Actros fully loaded with logs, parked up for the night in the market square. It was unusual to see a heavy haulage truck parked here and I rushed over to the nearby flat to get my camera since the rig looked good under the lights. The machine was run by BM. & R. Stephenson of York. As I was composing the shot, a lady of retirement age came up to me and said "I'm glad you're taking that picture". When I enquired why, she obviously misunderstood my innocent motive completely and went on to explain that she objected to such a vehicle parked where it was, disturbing the peace. She thought my photo might be used for some sort of spurious evidence for the authorities. No such thing – ever! On explaining this to Adam he told me that she was a recent 'blow-in' from a nearby town. Her husband formerly held some position of prominence and they sought to impose their busy-body ways on the market town. I've encountered this sort of thing before. Ironically, the driver would probably be up by 5am and gone, whereas the peremptory sheep-head looked like she'd never done a day's work in her life.

In November 1989 I was on foot walking through the Duddeston district of central Birmingham. I wasn't expecting much but thankfully I was ready with a camera and flash as this Leyland Marathon and chemical tanker flew by. BHA 597T was run by F&A Nixon Ltd of Oldbury and though not technically a great shot, it formed a characterful result on film. Digital is in many cases, so much better for low light with the camera hand held.

W.D. Cooper of Cannock ran a predominantly ERF fleet and I managed to capture most of their lorries from B Series onwards. I was passing by a large paper mill in the Saltley district of central Birmingham when I spied this pair of Cummins Super E14 E Series tractors loaded up in the fading light. March 1990 was the date.

119

This characterful working garage scene was up at Tinsley in Sheffield. Sidney Harrison and Sons let me loose in their yard back in December 1991 to capture their Gardner powered Scammell Highwayman tractors. I used a Practica BC1 camera and a 24mm wideangle lens on Kodachrome 64 film for the shot.

A Volvo F7 drawbar car transporter was parked up while loading in Great Barr Birmingham. The unit belonged to Kerling Transorters of Portsmouth was something I had not seen before. It was captured under fading light one late afternoon in January 1990.

With a long load of I-beam steel sections, this 1994 ERF EC Series twin-steer tractor was among the last of the marque using the composite constructed cabs and was very much a quality machine. JK Sturge of Stoke was the operator and they had run Bedfords in the past. The shot was taken around 2am in January 1999.

In the summer of 1990 I visited the premises of Beck and Pollitzer who had a depot in the Black Country district of Bilston. There was little heavy haulage in the yard, but I managed to get this well-worked 1981 Scania 141 V8 tractor in the garage. Flare from the overhead lighting was hard to avoid with my inexpensive twin-lens reflex camera.

121

This 1976 Volvo F88 operated by Roy Thomas of Morriston in Swansea was tipping a load of scrap metal around December 1989. The location was a yard in Wednesbury in the West Midlands and some flash helped illuminate the lorry in the dim winter light.

In 2016 I was visiting my daughter, Isabella in Toronto Canada. The summer months were a hive of building activity in the face of a severe upcoming winter freeze. I was enthralled by the 8-wheeled Mack DM and R Series concrete mixers which were commonplace around the city centre. This one, belonging to Canada Building Materials, required a shutter speed of 1/20th of a second to record the moving truck.

One winter around 1989 found me passing the yard of Kite Bros. Ltd of Netherton in Dudley. There were a few Bedford KM and TM rigids in the fleet in their regular green and red chassis colour scheme. Under the yard lights was this clean 1978 Leyland Marathon under contract I believe to C&S Steels of Bilston near Wolverhampton. The use of flash off-camera has rendered the blue on the cab correctly, to offset the amber street lamp.

In 1988 I managed to get an Atkinson Borderer on film and wanted to get a closeup. The following year I went to the premises of Stourbridge Stockholders Ltd on the edge of the town and was rewarded with this Guy Big J6 rigid dating from 1968. It was very cramped in their building, but I hunkered down and got the Guy's last hurrah before the scrapyard beckoned.

Sometime in the 1990s I went up to a boiler makers in Derby to photograph an ERF EC Series heavy haulage tractor operated by Starr Roadways of Bilston. As a bonus, this DAF 2800 was there so I took shots of this too. The driver skilfully coupled up to the heavily loaded trailer by reversing with a repeated 'clang' from the 5th wheel, to engage the tractor. I did wonder if it was up to the job without a broken chassis! The DAF was located at the Starr Leicester depot.

While reluctantly shuffling to the factory workplace in Erdington, Birmingham at 7.30am, I'd often have my camera ready in case anything interesting passed by on the busy Tyburn Road. This rare 1978 Volvo N10 fitted the bill and I think it was Derbyshire based. Luckily it was stuck in slow traffic so 1/125th of a second at f2.8 was enough to capture it in February 1988 near Spaghetti Junction.

EPILOGUE

I don't go out at night to take pictures like I used to. Sometimes it's time constraints but mostly I feel my work is done. It's similar to the photographers who wanted to record the last days of steam. There's no more Foden, Leyland and ERFs at night. Too many plain white lorries were starting to appear, although some better liveries abound on today's roads. More importantly, the environment has changed. Everything seems a bit more edgy. The proliferation of CCTV cameras, a 24 hour gym near where I used to take pictures and there's too many black BMWs with tinted windows around at 2am for my liking. On some of my last forays with my bike, occasional bold young ladies enquiring about 'business' would appear out of nowhere, giving me a start. A lorry driver with his window wound down arguing with someone over his mobile at 1am, less coppers around, more people taking and dealing drugs abounded etc. It's okay. We're all grown-ups. You can do what you like. But I'd rather not have to explain my benign activity to some sociopath with little empathy and an agenda. If it was scary before, its borderline terrifying now and I can involve myself in other creative endeavours that don't scare the bejesus out of me.

But sometimes I look at my bike at night, propped up and ready........

ABOUT THE AUTHOR

Mark Gredzinski has been photographing trucks for over 35 years and currently contributes to Heritage Commercials magazine. He has a BA Honours degree in photography, attained at Birmingham City University via Walsall College in 2015. Born in the working class district of Lozells, Birmingham, he has a lifelong interest in drag racing. He's worked for magazines such as Custom Car, Street Machine and American car world as a freelance photojournalist. Having trained as a silversmith and hand chaser, he developed an eye as both an artist and master model maker. He has won various awards for his illustrations and designs. Making entire engines from scratch, his models have appeared on the cover of various magazines. He also plays drums and percussion. And likes a real ale on occasion.

Nowadays you would call this a selfie. In July 1990 I'd taken a shot of a Tyson H Burridge ERF B Series twin steer tractor and decided to take a picture of myself. Really to kind of legitimise the fact that I was actually there in person, taking pictures as the sun went down when no-one was around.

The end of the book coincides with the end of a trailer. This picture depicts a pair of Blueline Transport lorries from South Wales. Heavily loaded with steel strip in the middle of the trailer, they were often part of a 3 or 4 truck convoy and March 1995 was the date for this shot of a Mercedes SK. Walsall Heat Treatment was the name above the open premises on the left and it was reassuring when the factory was on night shift, as I did not feel so vulnerable when photographing in the early hours.